A Perfectly Good Dog
Stories from the Heart

Grace Saalsaa

A Perfectly Good Dog

This collection copyright 1999 is by Grace Saalsaa

Acknowledgements

To my husband Dave
To Pallie, KC, Cap and Stevie Ray Dog

To my good friends, the S'Mores
Thanks for pushing me along

To my fellow rescuers
MidAmerica Border Collie Rescue
http://www.midamericabcrescue.com

Foreword

When Grace Saalsaa joined a Border Collie Email list, not many people took note at first. She would write telling a story about something that happened to her and her dogs. Later, the stories were also about the dogs she became involved with through various rescue groups.

People reading those stories gradually noticed that Grace's stories were something special. They started to look forward to her posts. After a while people begin suggesting that if the story was a sad one, she provide a tissue warning. Soon list members began requesting that Grace write a book, and they would repeat that request after almost every Grace story.

People began saving her stories and forwarding them to friends, and before long, Grace's stories were showing up on different sites around the Internet. Just type "Grace Saalsaa" in an Internet search and you will find her stories on many dog web sites. I have even received them as forwards, from a CAT list.

Grace's writing stirs an emotion in the reader. Her stories bring a smile, laughter, or tears, and animal lovers can relate to what she writes. She can put into words those things that other people feel or experience, but just can not express. Grace's sensitivity in dealing with animals makes the reader aware of what the dog must be feeling. As the Email list members say, "It's time for a Grace Story". Well, now it is time for a Grace Book!

- Mary Ann Sanford

Table of Contents

Awakening Consciousness

"**Why** do you think you need to do that?" my father asked of me at one time. He stood there in contraposto pose: hand on his hip, and casually looking down at my Border Collies.

He said he has always liked dogs – but I do not think the word "like" is the same to him as it is for me. He likes the look of a dog and the idea of companionship – but he does not like dog hair, vet bills, the daily need for attention, or the idea that somebody has to take care of The Dog. All those things amount to "bother" and a curtailment of freedom – and money spent on an...animal. However, he likes dogs - just as long as they are either outside or out of the way.

I, on the other hand, like dogs. I like feeling the gentle warmth leaning against my knee, the soft coat between my fingers, and the look of happiness in their bright eyes. I like watching them think and I like the way they "talk" to me. I thoroughly enjoy the

3

constant companionship of dogs, bother or no bother. I like dogs.

It is this "like" for dogs that brought me to where I am today. I have a deeper appreciation for all around me because a dog forced me to look at creation from a new perspective – one that focused on the sublime rather than materialistic desire. It is the perspective that, perhaps, a dog has. This perspective made me aware of how human I am and how inhumane my species can be.

I became a rescuer of dogs, and Border Collies is my breed of choice.

Sam stood on the green space between the large parking lot and the circular drive. Cars passed in all directions on this busy Sunday morning. She looked frazzled, and I wondered if she were a bit annoyed with me for being fifteen minutes late.

On the other end of the double leash, a dusty, black Labrador Retriever stood. His tongue hung long and limp like a deflated balloon. Sam looked slightly out of breath, just like the lab, and her eyes appear just the tiniest bit wild.

I rolled my white van to a stop next to her, and called out the window.

"Hi! You must be Sam. I'm sorry I'm late."

"Oh, that's ok. You must be Grace. Thank you so much for meeting me here. I just had the scare of my life!"

"What happened?" I asked as I stepped out of the van.

"The ring on this dog's collar broke, and he took off! Headed for the highway!" She pointed to the interstate not more than two blocks away. This is a rescuer's nightmare: transporting a dog you do not know, who does not know or trust you, and who does not know his name – and then something unforeseen happens. The collar breaks.

"Fortunately, he came right back to me. But God! My heart was in my throat!"

We chatted for a few minutes, and Sam brought out the second lab. Both dogs had just come from the Humane Society and were now headed for Lab Rescue. I was part of the transport connection that would help these two dogs get across the state and meet up with the next leg of their transport.

I stood there studying the two dogs. Both were too thin. Ribs protruded, and the dogs panted their stress. Totem, the smaller of the two, appeared to be in a weaker physical condition than Dietz. However, the thing they had in common, besides the bony bodies, was the look in their eyes. Any rescuer knows what I am talking about: that look in their eyes.

That look is a mixture of physical fatigue or illness and stress, coupled with helplessness and lost hope. Someone had loved them when they were plump little black puppies, squirming with happiness, sweetly innocent, and still smelling of "puppy breath." However, somewhere along their life's journey, something went wrong and the dogs lost their families.

"You'll never see your family again. It does not matter, Dog, that you loved them and needed them. It does not matter that you miss them tremendously or that you cannot understand what went wrong. You will never see them again. It will not help to mourn for them. Put away the sadness in your eyes. Rebuild your hope. You are headed for a new life. This new life will be better." The Rescuer softly stroked these thoughts into the dog's body while picking up the broken pieces of a dog's heart.

"We, as a society, fail in our responsibilities to those creatures that are our charges." It was this thought that once again awakened within me as I looked into the sad eyes of these two black labs. I felt sad to see them mourn, sad at their distress, and wished I could tell them today was the start of their new lives.

We, as a society, have become one that is tuned in to the quick and easy solutions. Time, comfort, money and freedom appear to be the most important considerations for many. There is nothing wrong with this - but when these considerations become so important that they outweigh the responsibilities, then something is not quite right. It is the difficult moments in life, the stresses and worries, love, and the responsibilities, that build character. Love and responsibilities, like the Border Collie, come in many forms. Sometimes it is as obvious as black and white and it wears a wagging tail.

The two black Labs lay quietly in their crates, staring out at me, unaware of the enormous change that was about to happen to their lives. I smiled and reached a finger into each crate to touch their black leathery noses. A new life was about to begin... new love and new happiness.

"Well Sam, it was a pleasure to meet you. Thank you for all you do. I have to go, though. I have a tri-colored Border Collie who is coming up from southern Kentucky today, and I am going to be late again, for that meeting. Best wishes to you Sam!"

"Same to you, Grace! Bye!"

Moaki and Her Pup

I doubt that we would ever have gotten a dog if it had not been for the Border Collie we found lying on the side of a country road one wet summer morning. This was the start of the adventure that eventually led me to Border Collie rescue. He was not injured; he was just tired because he was an old dog. We kept him for four days before his rightful owner found our ad in the paper and picked him up again on a Wednesday afternoon.

By then, we had a leash, collar, dog dish and big bag of dog food. We had the very basic things that said we owned a dog – except we did not have a dog.

On Thursday, Joe, a hippy carpenter friend of ours, stopped in for a visit and announced he had a Border Collie named Moaki. She was two years old and recently had a litter of eleven puppies. He asked us if we wanted a puppy. They were now eight weeks old and ready for adoption. They were free to a good home.

"You can have first pick of the litter," he said.

We arranged to go visit the following Sunday. Joe would not be home, however.

"That's ok. Just go to the back of the house. I'll leave the door open for you. Moaki and her puppies are in the greenhouse.

I was excited. I hadn't had a dog since I left home for college - and now I would have a dog of my own. It would be mine, not mom and dad's dog. Mine. I would care for it as I felt a dog should be cared for. Sunday, we piled into the jeep and headed out toward the lake where Joe lived.

An estimated ten thousand years ago, the lake had been created by the movement of a glacier, which resulted in sandy hills, flat outwash plains of rich black loam, drumlins and eskers, and a thick forest that covered the banks of the lake on all sides like the fluted crust of a pie. Running through the forest, fifty-five feet below the surface snaked an underground river that surfaced occasionally as an artisan well. People drove into the area from miles around with plastic jugs of all sizes and took home the icy cold water. "The magic water," they called it. It was always icy cold, tasted of iron, and surfaced not too far from Joe's home.

On hot summer days, I would take a jaunt out to Natureland where the water comes to the surface. Flowing out from under the roots of an ancient oak tree, the water pooled and formed a quiet little creek of very cold clean water, and then found its way into the lake.

8

When the opportunity presented itself, I threw off my shoes, socks, and stepped into the sandy-bottomed creek. The water just barely came up to my ankles. With a thin little stick in my hand, I would push away the occasional leeches that floated in the little eddies around the roots. Nope. I do not like leeches.

The narrow road out to Joe's house wound through the forest and over quick hills. Little roads seemed to wander off to nowhere, then found their way back to the shore. It was a peaceful day – a good day to meander the quiet roads, and a good day to take home a puppy.

As could be expected, Joe's house looked like the home of a free spirit. The four-foot wire fence that surrounded the yard attempted to contain the lawn – which had not been mowed all summer. Now standing three feet tall, the grass waved its tassles and leaned with the light summer breeze that rolled off the lake.

Sitting in the midst of the tall grass on the north end of the "lawn," sat a big yellow school bus.

"Naw. That's not a school bus," Joe said with a smile. "It's a storage unit." Indeed, the interior held an odd assortment of objects that truly did indicate this to be a storage unit: furniture, pipes, wood, and whatnot.

We waded through the tall grass, down to the backside of the house to the greenhouse, shaded by the Honey Locust trees nearby. The glass panes were faintly green and streaked with old dirt. I stood for a moment admiring the gentle shape of the greenhouse and thinking how lovely to have an addition such as this. Too bad Joe was not really using it as it was intended. Oh, well, perhaps he does when there are no puppies. Attached to the house, the greenhouse entry was through the back door. Sure enough, Joe had left the door unlocked for us.

We stepped into the cool interior of what appeared to be the living room. Sunlight followed us into the dim room and revealed a layer of dust on the hardwood floor. Footprints showed the pathway

9

from the greenhouse to the back door. There were footprints from work boots, and Moaki's paw prints. In the middle of the room stood a low footstool with a large white drop cloth hanging over one end. It was the only piece of furniture in the room.

At the sound of our footsteps, Moaki scrambled out from under the white drop cloth and met us at the back door. Obviously, this was where she spent time away from the puppies. She was slim and light on her feet, classically marked, and so alert. What impressed me the most was her dark brown eyes. They were deep with intelligence, and behind those eyes, her mind was busy thinking, thinking, thinking.

I reached a hand out to her, and with a big smile, she leaned up against my knees. Her coat was as soft as rabbit fur and radiated her youthful health. She seemed to know that we were here to meet her puppies, and she led the way into the greenhouse with a quick glance back at us.

All black and white, squirming and rolling about, they were so cute. To my biased mind, there is nothing as cute as a Border Collie puppy. (They remind me of tiny panda bears at this point in their development). Dave and I tried to study each puppy – but it was impossible because the puppies kept moving about.

"Did we look at this one yet?"

"I don't know…"

"Oh, look at that one!"

Dave squatted down next to the black cast iron skillet that was contained a mixture of kibble, vegetables and meat. One little puppy was rooting under the kibble to get at the mashed potatoes beneath. Although we had been examining the puppies for perhaps twenty minutes, this little puppy had completely ignored us. Standing with her tiny front paws in the black skillet, she was busy.

Dave picked her up and she squirmed with her hind legs dangling in space, and she growled her annoyance at being disturbed.

10

Her markings were the closest to being symmetrical.   She eyed us with a cool attitude, knowing in her little puppy mind that she was something special, and all the while a white glob of mashed potato sat on her nose. I smiled at her attitude and noted the keen intelligence and attitude behind her eyes – just like her mother's eyes.

The white glob of mashed potatoes and the fine intelligence in her eyes did it for me. I knew she had to be mine, and I suspected living with her would be an interesting journey. We let her finish her meal, picked her up, and carried her to the back door.

Moaki met us with suspicion, aware that we had one of her babies. I knelt on the floor beside her and spoke quietly to her while Dave carried the puppy outside.

"Moaki, is it ok with you if I take one of your babies home with me? I promise I will love her and care for her just as carefully as you have. You have ten other babies to care for. I would be honored to take care of this one for you."

Her head cocked from one side to the other as I spoke, and I could see all the intelligence behind her rich brown eyes again. She appeared to be considering this. Then she flipped her head back to the greenhouse, her tail wagged, and she trotted off to take care of the ten puppies. She had decided it was a good plan: she keeps ten puppies and I keep one.

I named my puppy Paloma, which means dove in Spanish. However, the name immediately shortened itself down to Pallie. Truly, this is the perfect name for her. She has been my constant companion, my love and my soul mate. She is a comfort when I need it, she keeps me on schedule, and on one occasion, she probably saved my life.

Because of her, I took up running and rediscovered how much I enjoy being outdoors. It is because of her I learned about Border Collies, and eventually her life, her energy, her pride and beauty encouraged me to because a rescuer of Border Collies.

11

To date, thirty-eight Border Collies have been guests here in my home. Pallie, with gray beginning to show around the corners of her mouth and eyes, now twelve years old, has been the Grand Mom, the Fun Police, and the one who teaches these foster dogs their dog manners.

Quietly, she lies by my feet whenever she can, and all I have to do is drop my hand to feel the heat of her head in my palm. With fur as soft as a rabbit, she emits great comfort, radiating love and a wisdom that extends beyond the both of us. There is only one dog like this one for me. It is my great fortune to be the one person with whom she wishes to walk life's journey.

Dream Story

With great heaviness of heart, she slowly lowered herself into her favorite chair. As the shadows of the evening covered her shoulders, she sat reflecting on that life. It was gone now. It had been so brief, so happy and filled with smiles, worries and mysteries. It was too brief. She was not ready for this to have happened. In her heart, she knew there was nothing else she could have done to change the outcome - but she was not ready for this.

She sank deeper into her chair, letting her hand drop over the side to reach for the soft warm head that had always been there before. Tonight she felt alone. She felt tired.

Ever so slowly, the room darkened and the sounds of her everyday world began to fade away as peaceful sleep wrapped its comforting arms around her. Her muscles relaxed, the warmth returned to her cold fingers and the sense of Another came to her. It guided her to that other place that she had always known about - but tonight it was somehow different. And after this night, it would always be different.

In the gentle quietness of her dreams, the portal of the dream world slowly and delicately unfolded like the most beautiful of exotic flowers. She felt herself gasp as the sheer loveliness and the harmony of it drew her forward.

Stepping through the portal of the Dreamworld, she found herself standing in a large open field. The fine music of the wind against her cheek whispered peace. Above her, she saw the bluest, purest sky she had ever seen.

Then a very familiar sound came to her. Her mouth gaped open in sheer delight as she watched her friend gracefully leap through the tall grass. With tongue flying backward, her friend's eyes shown brightly. There was a happiness that she had not ever seen before. The silky coat radiated health and well being as the dog effortlessly glided across the field to sit before her. All signs of pain and unhappiness were gone and in its place were strength, confidence and the Joy of Being.

"Oh, my love!" she said, "I thought you were gone! I tried so hard to keep you - to keep you safe and happy. I tried so hard - but then you were gone.... and I've missed you so." She knelt, buried her face and filled her hands with the softness of her friend's fur. And then, to her utter surprise, the dog spoke!

"No, dear mistress, I haven't left you. I am still here and I will always be with you. I'm in your shadow, I'm in the sunlight that caresses your skin, I'm in the scent of your favorite flower, I'm part of your hopes.... and I'm in your dreams. On the other side of this portal, I could see what you could not and heard the call that you missed. I could smell the sweetness of these meadow

14

flowers and with my keen eyes; I caught the vision of this perfect world.

From this side of the portal, I see you very clearly and I hear your thoughts. From this side, I understand what it is you have always said to me with your heart. I cannot go back through this portal - but you can come to spend your dreamtime with me. Here, neither one of us has pain or age to slow us down. Here, we share the same spirit and only here, you and I can speak to each other with the same language.

On this side of the portal, I will be your teacher. It will be my greatest joy to show you how to fly. We can laugh and run together. You and I."

When morning came, the sunlight gently kissed her skin and she woke with a smile, feeling such peace. Her friend had gone to a good place. Really, it wasn't so far away at all. It was just beyond the portal to the dream world.

A Perfectly Good Dog

KC's Story

It was a gray and windy morning. The sun remained buried behind a heavy ceiling of overstuffed clouds, and the threat of more rain still hung in the damp air. The wind slapped my hood against the back of my head and pushed me down the sidewalk. I skirted the puddles and the fat earthworms that blindly crawled across the pavement. I was deep in thought. My mood was as gray as the sky, and my mind had wandered forty miles away, to the university vet hospital. KC was there. Again.

My cell phone rang. It was the fourth-year student from the university veterinary hospital assigned to KC. She asked if I had gotten the message yesterday about the emergency surgery on another dog, and their not getting around to doing KC's surgery.

"First thing Thursday morning," the orthopedic surgeon had said about KC's surgery.

He had begun limping on the previous Wednesday. On Thursday, his hips were x-rayed and we discovered the artificial socket was broken. I could hardly believe it had happened again. This was the second time, and now I expected this would be viewed as a far more serious problem. Bits of cement floated around the joint, and the leg

17

was definitely out of the socket. Why did this happen? How did this happen?

The university veterinary hospital could not see KC any sooner than Monday on the following week. Surgery was supposed to have been first thing Tuesday morning.

Yeah well... "Thursday" - I guess not. Things change.

Sara, the fourth-year veterinary student called to say that the surgeon only works a half day on Thursdays and he didn't want to do KC's surgery tomorrow. (After all, it might cut into the second half of his day. Cannot have that). He wanted a big enough block of time to do KC's surgery. Seems to me, if he knows he does not have anything scheduled at the hospital for the second half of the day, then he did have that big block of time. Perhaps my logic is twisted...

"First thing Friday morning," she said.

Sigh.

Pallie and Cap trotted along quietly on the end of their leashes and stopped occasionally to grab a quick mouthful of couch grass. It was spring, and the couch grass was at its peak.

We've often seen dogs eating grass – but if you were to watch them closely, you would see that they are quite selective about the grass, and their favorite tends to be couch grass – also called quack grass. It is an herb, actually. In times of famine, the root has been roasted and ground to be used as a substitute for coffee and for flour. Juice from the roots, having a sweet almost licorice taste, has been used to treat jaundice, enlarged prostate, and other liver conditions.

Taken as a decoction over several months, the juice can help dissolve kidney stones. The extracts have antibiotic against bacteria and

18

mold, and it is rich in vitamin A, C and the B complexes. Couch grass also contains small amounts of calcium, and magnesium. Most commonly, couch grass is used for assisting the body in the inflammatory conditions caused by urinary tract infections. Dogs tend to eat it when they have an upset stomach – or just because they enjoy having the occasional "salad."

I turned my thoughts back to KC and watched him grab another blade of grass. He was happy for now. He turned his face toward me, a green slip of the grass hung from his chin, and his tail wagged. Little did he know what was in store for him once again. This would be the third hip surgery.

A large black lab came rushing up to a chain link fence, startling Cap, who reacted by running to the very end of his leash and nearly yanking me off my feet. I had almost forgotten I was outside walking the dogs, so engrossed was I in this phone conversation.

"Would you remind repeating that? It sounded like you said Friday morning." I pulled Cap back to my side and watched the lab trot off stiff-legged.

"Yes, first thing Friday morning. The doctor wants to have a big block of time set aside for KC since removing the implants will take some time. I also wanted to know what you feed KC. I've been trying a bunch of different dog foods and he hasn't eaten any of it."

"I feed him a raw diet."

"Ohhh... ok. I have some boiled chicken and rice. I'll try that."

A pause.

"You know what," I said, now not entirely comfortable about leaving KC at the university veterinary hospital. "How would it work if I could just bring him home today and then bring him back on Friday morning? He's not eating and that means he's stressed out. Since you

19

aren't doing surgery today - or tomorrow - there isn't anything different you can do that I wouldn't already be doing. In fact, KC will probably do better here with me than there with you."

"OK. That's fine – and I think you are right about that. KC really doesn't like being here, poor fella. I can see that he's trying to be brave about all this – but he knows what's going on. And he's done this before. I'll meet you in the lobby. What time do you think you'll be here?"

"I can be there in about an hour and a half. Thanks Sara. "

Sara just happened to be in the lobby when I walked through the door of the university veterinary hospital two hours later. Knowing how busy the veterinary hospital is, I truly did not expect her to be standing there.

"Oh! Hi Mrs. Saalsaa. I'll be with you in just a couple minutes." She disappeared down a hallway followed by a worried-looking man walking an old dog with a shaved groin and a green bandage around one paw.

I sat down facing the dogs' scale on the opposite wall, to wait. Loud sniffing sounds erupted in my left ear, and I turned to find a Briard standing on the bench behind me, unexpectedly finding myself nose to nose with him. The dog backed away and I became aware of all the other dogs in the lobby. I was not the only one worried about a beloved furry friend. It was a reality check.

A well-dressed woman against the far wall held a large mutt on a short leash. She reached over every few seconds to pat her dog's side. An old basset hound whined and paced continuously while his ears dragged the floor. Against the window, a woman sat with an empty leash and collar, wringing them together nervously. A couple sat nearby with a fat Sheltie in the man's lap. He kept telling her how much he loved her, and carefully rubbed a gnarled finger around the shaved and swollen scar on the sheltie's head. Cancer. The Briard was now snorting. He had a nasal tumor. Yes, a reality check. I am not the only person in the lobby who loves her dog sincerely.

I neglected to bring a book with me, and the well-thumbed magazines scattered about the lobby did not look a bit interesting. Once again, my mind wandered – but this time it was back to the first year that KC had come to live with us...

At one time in KC's history, somebody had driven him far from home, removed his collar and tossed him out of the moving vehicle. Tumbling and rolling he came to a stop, feeling pain after pain shift about his body. His jaw hurt and his head began to ache from the additional pain in his twisted neck. Each breath came with difficulty because four ribs had popped out of place, and each step hurt. His had injured his paws as well.

I can visualize the trust that KC had had in this person and the fear that must have followed as he struggled to run after the disappearing car. He was a young adult – not much more than a big puppy. He was alone now, with no experience at being alone. He was lost and frightened. The last contact with his owner had been the removal of his collar, and that fateful car ride.

Several weeks went by, and KC wandered through the streets searching out food and water, lying down under bushes for the night, as

21

he struggled to make a new life for himself. Reports began coming into the shelter of a very skinny stray dog wandering through the area.

"He's really friendly – but he's so skinny and scared. "

My thoughts were interrupted when Sara returned with KC. He looked tired and worried. KC pulled to get to the doors. I'm sure he thought he was going out for a potty break. So intent on heading outside, he ignored everything about him. His front paws slid on the tile flooring. The doors opened to let a man in with a huge Leonberger. KC's eyes focused on the dry leaves that scuttled in the door, and not once did he look in my direction.

"KC, look who's here!" Sara said.

KC pulled to get to the door. I stood up and called his name as I walked to him. To anyone else in the lobby, KC looked sleek and soft, quiet dog with a handsomely gentle face. Nothing wrong with him ... except for that limp. No shaved areas on him... yet. His head pulled up and the worried expression immediately vanished. He ears folded neatly behind his head, and his tired eyes lit up with joy. He wagged his entire body and strained to push his head into his collar the moment I pulled it from my pocket.

"See you Friday morning, Sara," I said as I led KC out the door.

KC immediately began crying as we walked through the parking lot. He looked at each parked car, and pulled to get to the green jeep the moment he found it. The entire trip home he sat huddled in the crate, panting and trembling. However, when we got to the downtown section of our city and were just about four blocks from home, he realized where we were. All the trembling and worry disappeared.

I do not know who has happier: KC or Dave. Dave knelt on the floor and threw his arms around KC, so relieved to have him back again. Sad thing, though. KC was to go back on Friday. At least the two of them were happy. KC sprawled out on the floor by Dave's fee,; sound asleep, with his hip still broken.

First thing Friday morning...

When we discovered that KC had Canine Hip Dysplasia, our hearts sank. Everyone told us to put him down. He is too skinny, he has dead-looking fur, and we could replace him with another dog. However, it is impossible for me to just put down a young dog that looked at me with those soft brown eyes burdened with pain, telling me he hurts, and smiling at the same time.

Everyday as I worked at my desk, he would come to me quietly, nudge my elbow, and then position himself for a massage. This would happen at least a dozen times a day. He understood that I knew he was in pain. He also knew that I knew exactly where it hurt.

In the evenings, he would lie down and struggle to find the least painful position for his hind legs. When he got up, he held his right foot about an inch off the floor for about a minute, until the pain eased up. Sometimes, especially on cool, damp evenings, he would put his head on the couch. I knew he wanted to jump up but he just did not want to subject himself to the extra pain. Therefore, looking very tired, he would stand there with his chin on the couch.

We took him and his x-rays to the veterinary hospital in Madison, Wisconsin and consulted the orthopedic surgeon. KC is afraid of long drives. The forty-five minute drive had him huddled in the back seat with his face in the corner, unresponsive and trembling.

I wondered if it was a leftover worry from the nine-hour trip we took to get him. When he left his happy foster home, he left his playmates, the foster couple that he loved, a familiar routine, and a familiar place. KC loved his foster dad, and the smooth-coated Border Collie, named Chase – also a foster dog – was his best friend.

All smiles and happiness, KC had greeted us at the door, and then threw himself into Dave's lap as though to claim:

"This is my human."

I smiled as I remembered the "work" KC and Chase had done in the kitchen. Brad had gone to the lumberyard to pick up the materials for the new gate to the backyard. The screen door had the bottom panel missing, and when the dogs went out, all Brad had to do was open the inside door. The dogs stepped through the missing panel and freely romped about the long backyard.

Figuring he would not be gone too long, he left the door open to the yard. However, the trip took a little bit longer than he had expected. The two young Border Collies got bored, and one of them pulled up the loose corner of the linoleum flooring right in front of the door.

As can be expected from a Border Collie, considered the most intelligent breed, boredom leads to getting "unbored." In addition, a bored Border Collie can be rather destructive. The two dogs removed a four foot square piece of the linoleum and carried it into the backyard where they made confetti out of it. There was not a piece bigger than a thumbnail. Next, they removed a three-foot length of wooden trim from both sides of the door. Finally, Brad came home.

"It was entirely my fault," Brad said sheepishly. "I had to wait at the lumberyard, and it took longer than I expected. I guess I'll be going back to the lumberyard for some new kitchen flooring and some trim for the door." He scratched the back of his head and gave me a little grin.

We named him Kansas City Dog, filled out the adoption contract, and KC hopped right onto my jeep. Sitting there in the middle of the back seat, he waited for Brad to get in too. He had a big smile on his face and his tail flopped up and down on the car seat.

"Oh no," Brad eyes were rimmed in red and his voice grew husky. "He's been my buddy...loves me – and he's not going to understand why he won't ever see me again."

That happy young dog now lay sprawled tight to the car seat, panting heavily. There was no joy here now for him. At one point during the trip back to Wisconsin, he realized his life was about to change. He looked at me as though to say: "I don't know you. I'm not sure I can trust you."

I also wondered if he was having a flashback and the memory of being tossed out of a vehicle had him this upset. There was no way to console him. If I reached over and touched him, he would dig his nails into the car seat and get as low as possible. The towel beneath him was damp with saliva, and by the time we arrived at the veterinary hospital for the consultation, KC looked exhausted.

The surgeon told us KC was possibly too young for surgery. Even if he were old enough, he was too skinny and he not healthy enough to survive the hip surgery. The hips were indeed very bad, and we should wait. But could we wait?

"I can do the surgery at any point in KC's life. But right now, I don't think he is in that much pain."

We told the surgeon that we would be back when KC was a little older, healthier, and had reached the recommended weight of forty

25

pounds. His estimated ideal weight was forty-seven pounds. However, right now, he would need to put on eight pounds to reach the recommended weight of forty pounds for surgery.

KC took pain medication for a month, and it helped. We gave him glucosamine and that appeared to help as well. Yet, he had to endure a lot of pain. In the evenings, when his pain was more than he wanted to endure, he came to me with his droopy ears, sad eyes, and nudged me repeatedly. I could see that he was very tired, and I know that pain can be exhausting.

KC wanted to sleep but the pain would not let him. I laid him gently on his side and wrapped a long rectangular heating pad around his hips. While the heat soaked in, I gently massaged his hips, the leg muscles and a broad area above the base of his tail, and up his back. He would let out a sigh and fall into a deep peaceful sleep.

I began to wonder: how much pain must he endure? How much was enough? The surgeon said that KC would tell us when he had had enough pain and to wait until then. However, as I thought about it, I realized that KC had been telling us all along he had had enough. KC was four months older now, weighed thirty-nine pounds, nine ounces, and he was otherwise healthy. There appeared to be nothing wrong with this young Border Collie except his hips - and this surgeon said these were fixable.

Yes, the surgery could wait until KC was five years old - but he would have to go through four years of pain. In addition, all that wonderful puppy silliness would have been lost. All the play and joy of discovery would be dampened. His quality of life would have been less than it could be. I thought to myself that it was unfair and selfish of me to make him suffer when I was the one who had to decide how much pain he should endure. We made the appointment for his total hip replacement.

On a Monday, I picked KC up, put him in the car and drove to Madison again. KC huddled in the back seat trembling with his head tucked into the corner of the seat again. He was full of fear. I wished Madison were not forty-five minutes away.

Three surgeons and a fourth-year student examined KC by laying him on his side and tested his range of motion. I knew this was painful for him, but he is such a stoic dog, he only whimpered once. When he got to his feet again, he wagged his tail, gave everyone his sweet sad smile, gently licked the closest hand, and then leaned against me for comfort. He was frightened but he put his best face forward, and he could endure it all because he knew that I was there with him.

They would remove the femoral head and the core of the femur would be drilled and enlarged to accept the implant. A synthetic cup would be placed into a created space in the pelvis and would be come his new hip socket. The surgeon told me that KC had slender bones. The problem he foresaw was the possibility of shattering the femur when he pushed the leg into the new socket. This would be very bad. The surgeon asked me what I wanted him to do. I said:

"Do a total hip replacement. But if you see that this would be unwise when you get in there, then do a Femoral Head Osteotomy." So it was decided.

KC stood quietly beside me while the fourth-year student unhooked his leash and petted him. Then he removed KC's collar and handed it back to me, saying that they would use a plastic collar without metal on it during KC's stay at the hospital.

The last contact with his previous owner had been the removal of his collar. Now his collar was being removed again. The look on KC's face suddenly registered that he remembered.

KC looked up at me as I held his beloved collar - his sense of security – in my hand. I watched his ears droop. He looked me straight in the eye and that look on his face said:

"I trusted you. I thought you loved me."

Slowly his head began to droop too and the light of joy and life and hope and happiness in his eyes began to grow dim. He let out a pathetic little sigh and turned away from me.

"Oh no," I cried. "He thinks he is at an animal shelter again! He thinks I'm leaving him." Everybody in the room got misty-eyed. "Oh...KC."

I knelt on the floor and wrapped my arms around him. For a brief moment, his body relaxed and he leaned into me. Then he stiffened, refused to look at me anymore and held his stoic little head high.

"KC," I whispered into his droopy ear, "Its just for a little while. I promise you, my little one: I will never desert you. You can depend on me."

However, KC did not understand a word I was saying, and they led him away. They took him out into another room that smelled of illness and fear. It was a room that echoed with the cries of loneliness. I stood there with the empty collar in my hand, still warm from his body heat and shiny on the inside from the oils in his coat. The tags that said, "My name is KC. I belong to Grace & Dave Saalsaa." They jingled as I fumbled to hold onto the collar.

In the car, I turned on the wipers and then turned them off again when I realized that the blurry vision was not rain on the windshield. What had I done?! What if the surgery went bad and KC died? My last memories of him would be that look he had given me - and holding the empty collar. The next four days were anxiety-ridden.

On Thursday, Dave and I took the morning off to bring KC home. Surgery had gone very well except that KC had thrashed about coming out of the anesthetic, and they had x-rayed his hip again for fear that he might have dislocated it.

The hospital lobby had tile flooring, which can be slippery for an excited dog. The fourth-year student took KC, supported by a towel sling, out to the sidewalk, while the surgeon walked us out another door for the reunion.

KC stood there looking pleased to be out of the kennel and in the cool breeze. I could tell he was not entirely happy. No family anymore - but at least he was outside and away from the sights, sounds and smells inside. He turned his head toward us when he heard the surgeon's voice but did not recognize us. He thought we were gone for good.

As the wind blew past us and rolled down the sidewalk toward him, his head popped up and his nose began to quiver. He swung his head about, fixing us with an intense Border Collie "eye," and he looked utterly delighted. I pulled his beloved collar from my pocket and held it up for him to see. His ears popped up, and a big doggy grin covered his face while he stretched and strained to get his head into the collar.

"Let's go home, KC!"

It was now Friday morning, six years later. The university veterinary hospital was springing to life. Doctors and other staff were just arriving. Many carried a briefcase in one hand and a mug of coffee in the other. Some looked tired already, and I imagined they were thinking,

"Thank God it"s Friday."

Apparently, KC's surgery was a big deal. The hospital does not schedule surgeries on Friday – but KC's broken acetabular cup was unusual since this was the second time he had broken it. This would be KC's third hip surgery, and he was the first dog to undergo a third hip surgery.

Now at a trim and healthy forty-five pounds, one would expect that this would not happen to a Border Collie... perhaps a larger, heavier breed – but not a slender Border Collie. KC's surgery was going to be in the larger operating theater where the veterinary students could watch and learn. The three senior orthopedic surgeons would be present for the surgery. Nothing else had been scheduled for the entire morning in the orthopedics department - just KC's hip surgery, and they expected it to take up to five hours.

The surgeons had already informed us that they would not replace the broken acetabular socket, and if KC needed hip surgery on his other hip, they would not do a total hip replacement. KC had only two options left: remove all the hardware, or euthanize him. Obviously, we were not about to euthanize him because he was otherwise a healthy dog.

The surgeons had carefully explained the surgery. They would saw a "window" into the femur, grasp the end of the implant, and pound it up and out of the bone, hoping that the cement that held it in place would break away easily. Their concern was if the femur were to shatter, a plate and pins would have to be implanted to repair the broken bone. If the bone shattered, it would be a long and nasty surgery. The acetabular cup was already loose, and it would pop out easily.

However, for the veterinary students, it would be a rare and exciting event to watch. I was sure they would be video taping the surgery to use later as a learning tool. Yes, my dog was a learning tool. I hoped the surgeons would not become so involved in the technical aspects of teaching and doing this "unusual" surgery, that they would forget he was also My Dog.

KC was not happy to be back at the university hospital again. However, he accepted his fate and smiled bravely as the fourth year student led him back into the bowels of the building.

I walked slowly to my car and stood for a moment with my hand resting lightly on the latch. The parking lot was beginning to fill up. People walked into the building carrying small cat crates or dogs on leashes. I studied their faces and saw bravery, fear, worry, anger, tears, and stony silence. I was reminded once again that I was not the only person with a greatly loved companion animal.

Putting aside worries, I turned my back on the veterinary hospital and watched two ducks float lazily down the creek. It was a peaceful sight and I felt the tensions melt away. I drove home to wait for a phone call from Sara or one of the surgeons.

"Hi Mrs. Saalsaa. It's Sara! I have good news for you. KC's surgery didn't take as long as they thought it would. He's out of surgery and is resting comfortably. The implant came out easily and everyone was surprised – but happy they didn't have to worry about shattered bones."

31

"Oh good! I am so relieved. When can I bring KC home?"

"Well, we'd like him to stay here today to make sure he comes out of the anesthetic safely – and he has a IV drip going. Pain meds, you know. I thought you'd be anxious to get him home, so I've already asked. You can come get him tomorrow morning as long as nothing unexpected happens today. Perhaps you should call in the morning before you leave town."

The next morning, I hopped in my jeep and once again, drove to the university veterinary hospital. A smile sat on my face the entire trip. I pulled into the empty parking lot, and glanced at my watch.

"OK. I'm a little early and nobody is here yet." I opened the book I had brought along and attempted to read. However, not a single word made the slightest comprehensive sense. My mind was inside the building, pacing the floor, and waiting for KC.

"I might as well get a cup of coffee."

A half hour later, I returned and the building was full of activity. The receptionist paged Sara, and a few minutes later, she walked into the lobby with KC. In her right hand was his leash and her left hand supported his hips in a fleece-lined sling.

KC knew he was leaving the hospital. This time, he fully expected to see me. I had promised that I would never abandon him, and each time he had come out of the veterinary hospital, I was there.

32

He swung his head about, scanning the benches in the waiting area, and all the faces. His nose quivered as he hunted for my scent.

A happy smile flooded his face the moment he spotted me. I knelt down on the floor and held my arms wide for him. He pulled against the sling Sara used to support his hind legs, and struggled to get to me as quickly as he could.

Once again, his hip was shaved down to the hock, making him look as though he were wearing a fuzzy sock. The long surgical line with bright metallic staples marched down his upper thigh, and stood out against his bluish skin. It was the third such line down his hip.

Sara handed me the artificial socket and the metal implant. I was not sure that they would keep them for me, but it is a bit of KC's history. I have no puppy pictures of KC, but I have these two very expensive bits of hardware…

KC pulled as much as he was able to, heading for the door – outside and away from this place! Unable to be brave any longer, he began crying. I opened the big glass door and KC scurried outside.

He searched the parking lot for my green jeep and hurried me along. There was clearly no doubt what he wanted. KC stood with his nose pressed against the crack of the closed door in an unfeigned desire to get inside, and he continued to cry.

"Let's go home, KC!"

I opened the door and carefully put him inside the crate. KC nestled himself down in the thick bedding and let out a sigh of relief. He closed his eyes, buried his face, and prepared himself for the long drive home.

A Guy and His Dog

A very nice person, named Greg, used to work for me. I hired him right out of high school - and two weeks after he started working for me, Dave (my husband) suddenly ended up in the hospital because he passed out about 2:00 in the morning. He spent about two weeks first in the local hospital and then, was transported by ambulance to a hospital in Milwaukee, known for its expertise in heart conditions. Every day for those two weeks, I left this 18-year-old kid alone to care for the whole store, and he was terrific. He was dependable, trustworthy, friendly, and a just an all around good kid.

Finally, when he turned 30, he moved on and got another job in a similar field. Greg still stops in every couple of weeks to chat with us when we take a coffee break. He still lives at the end of the block, across the street and up two houses. He remains the same amiable, outdoorsy person he was as a youngster, and a dog is just a natural extension of his personality. Greg was meant to have a dog, and any dog that came to be his would never be forgotten or neglected.

Here, my story begins.

Twelve years ago, when Greg had not yet moved out of his apartment, he decided that he really missed having a dog. Greg is big on hunting, and his dream was to have a bird dog again. Greg's dad had a female who was pregnant with her first, and only litter of puppies, and the thought of having a bird dog once again burned keenly in Greg's heart. Daily he would tell us how big the female was getting. It was easy to see how exciting this upcoming event was, and with it, the spark of dog ownership began to ignite within his heart. He really wanted a dog.

Late one night, Greg called quite excited, to say that the puppies had arrived during the late evening hours. He was tired but very happy.

All through the night puppy after puppy arrived, and Greg was right there helping with the delivery, checking them over, heart thumping with the thrill of these fragile, still sightless, little Chesapeake Bay Retriever pups. They were all fine, such splendid puppies. Oh... he wanted one of those puppies so badly. Against his better judgment, knowing that he lived in an apartment where he was not allowed to have a dog, he asked if he could have this lovely little female puppy.

Holding the tiny little puppy in his large hands, he felt the warmth of her tiny body grab hold of his heart, and with eyes closed, he gently pressed the puppy to his cheek. She was a fine puppy. He could imagine her pushing through the brush, flushing out birds, sitting in the duck blind with him, and lying by his feet in the evenings. Yes, she would be a fine hunting dog.

Greg's father, also very much a hunter and a dog person, agreed to give Greg the little female. The arrangement was made that Greg's little puppy would stay at his father's house and every day Greg would drive into town to take care of her.

I never thought this arrangement would work, but you know what? Greg was faithful to that puppy. There was not a day that went by that Greg was not there to care for his precious puppy. He loved her with all his heart and, being an avid sports fan, he named his new little puppy "Voja" after a hockey player.

Eventually the time came when Greg's dad could not keep Voja at his home any longer. I remember the sadness and the worry in Greg's voice as he told us about this unfortunate turn of events. Greg mulled over many outcomes, and the one that worried him the most was the possibility that he might have to give his dog away.

Instead, Greg sought some other means to keep his beloved Voja. His grandfather lived just about four miles east of town on a small farm, and agreed to let Voja stay at his place. Greg created large kennel space from the area between two out buildings. He bought the fencing, put down gravel and a doghouse. I never thought this arrangement would work, but you know what? Greg was faithful to his young dog. There was not a day that Greg was not there to take care of his precious Voja.

He would get out to the farm at 5 o'clock every morning and take Voja out into the fields to teach her the fine art of retrieving. Often I would see Greg and Voja coming back into town. He would wave cheerfully, and Voja would be standing in the passenger seat with the retrieving dummy hanging out the end of her mouth like a large swollen cigar. Often she was wet because they had been down to the lake for a lesson on retrieving game from the water. I would always smile to myself and think, "a guy and his dog."

In many ways, Greg regarded Voja as a more than just a dog - a working dog, yes, and as something else too. He also regarded her as a tool for hunting. However, I have to tell you, that when he came to work, he saw how Pallie and KC lived, thought, loved, and communicated with me. Subtly they influenced his thinking, and he changed Voja's diet.

"Cheap" dog food is actually not cheap at all. In the long run, it is more expensive. "Cheap" dog food contains more fillers - things that a dog cannot use as food, and protein of questionable nutrition.

Consequently, a dog living on "cheap" dog food has to eat more of it in order to get the nutrition it needs. Moreover, eating more dog food means there will be more poop pick up, a shorter life span, and perhaps even more vet bills. Good nutrition is necessary for growing a healthy brain and body. Without proper nutrition, a dog will be less than it could be.

Shortly after the dog food conversation, Greg told Dave and I that he had switched Voja to a better dog food and was astonished to discover she was eating half as much dog food, pooping half as much, and that the more expensive better dog food actually cost less because he didn't have to feed her as much of it. In return, Voja's coat grew shiny and healthier. Her eyes were brighter, and the fog that seemed to sometimes dull her intellect disappeared. She was happier, healthier and lovelier than ever. She was indeed, a divine dog.

I would tell Greg about some of the amusing stories of having a dog in the house. Perhaps at his home as a child, the family dog had lived outside - but still, it received the care and attention a dog should have: regular vet visits, daily romps in the fields and woods, and swims in the lake. During the winter, Voja's doghouse was insulated, and Greg put a flap over the door to keep the draft out. Extra bedding went onto the floor to keep the cold from creeping up from beneath.

Shortly after that, Greg and his wife moved into town. They found a house to rent at the end of the block, across the street, and two doors up from our house. For the first time, Greg could bring Voja home with him because the landlord was dog friendly, and a big time hunter himself. Soon, Greg just loved having a dog in the house, and had his own stories to tell. It was not long before Voja had her very own bedroom and her spot on the couch. She was happier than she could ever remember being.

Greg and Voja were kindred spirits. They both loved hunting birds. More than the hunting or anything else, they both loved being outside and being a part of nature. Swimming, hiking, taking long naps out under the shade of a pine tree in the middle of a broad expanse of prairie grass, a guy and his dog breathed and lived a happy life together.

Often I would see them coming back into town with Voja standing on the seat, a retrieving dummy protruding from the end of her mouth. Her body was wet and her face was still covered with extreme happiness. So was his.

Greg's large hands would sweep long strokes of love down her muscled body, and she would look up into his eyes with adoration. Voja was his dog - his soul mate, and she loved him more than she loved any human that ever existed. She lived her life to the fullest, and she lived it for him.

Voja had aged before Greg knew it. In his eyes, she was still the lovely female with the happy eyes; she was the dog who waited eagerly for him to come home each evening. When he was not home, she would wait for him, curled up in his chair where his scent was the strongest, for this was as close as she could be to him when he was not there.

Each evening she greeted him with happiness, and her genuine pleasure never failed to lighten the remainder of the day. Home is where the heart is - and Voja had his heart. The graying around her muzzle and the slowing down of her step went barely noticed because it is hard to see the love of your heart grow old.

Vaguely he became aware that she no longer wanted to climb the stairs to the bedroom. He would carry her upstairs. One day she whimpered with pain when he picked her up, and after that, he decided to bring her couch downstairs. She was getting stiff and there was a definite popping noise in her old hips. However, her tail always wagged for him and her eyes were still filled the love of twelve years. Gradually the thought began to press in upon him: she would not be here with him forever. Her life was limited.

One day Greg's wife called him while he was halfway up the state on business. She was very worried about Voja because she was not able to get up by herself, and she had not eaten her meal. Greg instructed Lisa to take Voja to the vet and to call him when she returned home. Well, the retuned phone call was not the happiest news. Sadly, Voja was experiencing liver failure - and she was dying.

Greg cut his business trip short, and drove home, arriving at 11:00 in the evening. Voja lay quietly on her couch, with her eyes fixed on the door. She had heard the hum of Greg's car and her tail began to wag as it always did. The love of her life - the love of her entire life - was finally home. How happy she was once again.

He knelt beside her and ran his warm hands down her tired body, running long strokes of all the love he had in him. She smiled, happy to know that he still loved her. It did not matter that she was old and tired, it did not matter that she could not retrieve anymore, and it did not matter than she could not go for those wonderful long hikes with him anymore.

Greg did not care about that because when he came down to it, what he really loved more than anything, was Voja. In his heart, she was still the most wonderful companion a fella could have.

She laid her copper-colored head, now peppered with white, on his forearm and wrapped a paw over his hand. She had waited for him to come home just one more time. With his head buried in the short curls of her withers, he laid his hand upon her side, and he cried many tears as he felt her body grow still for the last time.

I See You

I stood before the mirror and studied the frowning figure reflecting back at me. My favorite shirt, so baggy and comfortable, did nothing for me except make me feel comfortable … and baggy. The jeans were old with loose threads dangling around my ankles, and faded thin over the thighs. Poking over the top of my fuzzy blue slippers were wild-colored fleece socks.

I held a cup of hot cocoa in a large mug and studied my unkempt hair. I needed a haircut. It was either that or let it grow out and get an army of hairclips until it was long enough to pull back into a ponytail. A few white hairs along my temple stood out, and caught by the slight draft that wafted down the hallway, they shifted positions, reminding me of the "feelers" on a snail.

I turned sideways. This angle was worse. I sucked my stomach in and straightened my posture. It didn't help. I walked up closer to the mirror and studied my face. Each morning, I put make-up on. However, I never really looked at ME. What do people see when they look at me?

Did they also see black hair with white "feelers" floating about my head? Did they see a tired face with little creases across the forehead and age spots from spending so much time hiking outside on the forest trails? Would they notice the beginning signs of arthritis in my posture, the stiffness when I bend over or reach? Does anybody notice that I now hold things farther from my face in order to read?

Should I care? I never expected to age gracefully. I never expected to feel pretty and preserved when I took my last breath. I thought about a quote that was sent to me by a friend: I shall go out thoroughly used up, and hopefully feeling that I had made a positive difference in this world. This would be my measure of a successful life. As I skid and slide sideways into my grave, perhaps my last thought will be "wow, what a ride!"

A light clicking of toenails on the hardwood floor came down the hallway and stopped in the somber shadows. I turned to see Pallie nestle herself into a sphinx position with her face turned up at me. White hairs now framed the corners of her mouth. Her step is slower, and she prefers to observe life rather than chase it up a tree. Her chestnut-colored eyes are full of wisdom, and a love for me. She too, shows the signs of age. Yet, she wore it so beautifully.

"Why is it sweetie, that you still look so beautiful?" I laid down on the floor facing her, rested on my elbows, and lightly caressed Pallie's front paws. She reciprocated with kisses. "You're coat is still

40

luxurious and soft, your eyes show me your thoughts, and although your figure is a little fuller, it doesn't matter to me. You still are the most wonderful Border Collie I have ever met. You are my soul mate."

"Ah," said Pallie. "I was thinking nearly the same thing about you. When beheld as wonderful – successfully wonderful, it is best to wear your beauty on the inside. This is where I look when I see you – and this is where you look when you see me."

A Perfectly Good Dog

Good-Bye Old Friend

The day was hot and humid – and so very typical for the end of July. Fortunately, an efficient breeze prevented the insufferably damp air from thoroughly wrapping itself about me. I pushed the wild strands of hair off my cheek and squinted into the bright sun. Thank goodness, this was just a "potty break" and I was not actually going to have to be out here for any real length of time. I glanced down at KC, whose thick coat of slate gray fur seemed to be shielding him from the heat and humidity.

"Let's go, KC," I said, giving the leash a light flick.

KC had his leg hiked up and was leaving a message on the fire hydrant. I knew he would check out the opposite side of the hydrant next if I did not encourage him to move on.

He trotted off, leading me along George Street, which is a dead end lane. Half way down, the creek meets George Street and flows beneath it. It jabbered to itself as it dashed over the scramble of limestone rocks strewn about in the shallow end just beyond the bridge. The hill in the middle of the street sloped quickly away from the bridge and the grass turned a vibrant green, shaded in the cool created by the large willow trees. They hugged the bank with their gnarly roots dangling in the muddy creek. Fat catfish hid amongst the flowering

43

water plants, feeding and dozing in a rhythm that suited the flow of the creek and the lazy heat of the summer.

George Street is quiet and lined with large silver maples. Hardly a car passes by in the middle of the day, for the neighbors are all off to work. It is the perfect place to take KC for the mid day jaunt. We would walk down the length of George Street to the cul-de-sac at the end, cut across someone's side yard, and cross the creek again as it cuts a sharp curve before meandering its way back to the mill on First Street. KC settled into a trot, ticking out a cadence with his toenails.

It was garbage pick-up day. Our town is small enough that all trash is picked up on Thursday. By 2 o'clock in the afternoon, every trash container in town is empty, and the garbage trucks rumble their way out to the recycling center on the north end of the city.

The dark brown bin is for trash; the dark green is for recyclables.

KC and I slowed our pace with marked curiosity, as we approached a gray house on our left. The driveway had been recently retopped in a rich, black layer of asphalt. The house, freshly painted, also sported new crisp white curtains laced in splendid tatting.

There, at the end of the unsullied black driveway, pillared by the two trash bins, sat an old recliner. The headrest was stained and permanently impressed by the back of someone's head. The seat cushion bulged out of shape as though someone had a favorite position, which was not quite square with the shape that had been intended for the cushion. The footrest, with stuffing escaping from one end, gaped slightly outward as though someone intended to return shortly.

KC paused for a moment to check out the scent on the chair. I pulled him away quickly before he hiked his leg again and claimed the chair as his, and we moved along down George Street to the bend in the

44

creek.   Off in the distance, on the next block, the garbage trucks rumbled along.

On the return trip up George Street, the recliner was occupied. The summer breeze wafted over the figure of a rumpled man, deeply embedded in his old recliner, mouth slightly ajar, and snoring peacefully.   His T-shirt was unkempt as was his baggy checkered shorts. He just looked like he belonged with the recliner.

With his head nodded off to one side, and a leg thrown over the opposing chair arm, he slept soundly. Bare foot, one heel rested in the stuffing of the footrest, his right hand lay gently on top of a small cooler beside the recliner.   Yes, this explained the stains and the deformities to the recliner. It was obviously the man's favorite chair.

I glanced back at the crisp window curtains, the fresh paint, and began to suppose what might have gone on inside the house. The man had probably lost his argument on why he should be allowed to keep his chair. It was Thursday. It was garbage pick-up day, and today would be the last time he would be able to take a nap in his beloved recliner.

Situated between the two trash containers in the shade of the great silver maple, he quietly slept his last sleep in the old recliner. I smiled with amusement – and with just a pinch of sympathy for the man.

Ah yes. The garbage truck arrived as we approached from the opposite side of the street. With a hiss, and a puff of black smoke, it crawled to a stop beside the sleeping man in the recliner.

KC sat down and studied the sleeping man intently. Was the man going out with the trash too? Two big robust men popped off the truck and smiled at the sight of the sleeper in the recliner. They quietly removed the two trash containers, emptied them, and returned them to the side of the driveway. The sleeping man never noticed.

One of the garbage men slowly walked up to the recliner and nudged the sleeping man. His eyes opened with great difficulty, and as his vision shifted upward to the garbage man, a most pathetic expression descended over his quiet face. It was time. The end was here.

He pushed himself out of the chair, straightened his rumpled T-shirt, opened the cooler and produced a can of beer. With a flourish, he motioned the two garbage men to take his beloved recliner away. The can hissed and a fine spray of foam spurted over the recliner as the two big men lifted the chair into the back of the garbage truck.

Saluting the recliner with his can of beer, the man sobbed:

"Good-bye, old friend."

A Ghost Story

The Kettle Moraine State forest covers several thousand acres in the southeastern corner of Wisconsin. We live in the glaciated part of the state and are blessed to have this hilly forest just a 7 minute drive from my home. The hills can be long and twisting, bordered by steep potholes and kettles.

Sometimes you will suddenly find yourself on the top of ridge facing a grassy prairie. In some areas, if you dig down a foot, water fills the hole because there is an underground river that runs silently beneath the sandy soil, only surfacing occasionally to produce the trout streams and small lakes. The water is so icy cold that to stand barefoot on the sandy streambed will freeze your feet within minutes.

Ahh .... it is a wonderful thing to pull off your running shoes and sweaty socks on a hot hot summer day. Pushing your toes down into the sandy bottom to withstand the numbing cold of the flowing water while watching for bloodsuckers is such delicious torture.

During WWII, nearly all the trees were cleared and the Conservation Corp came through to plant pines again. If ever you find yourself lost in this vast forest, look for the pine trees that have been planted in rows. They run north and south. With that little bit of knowledge, you have to be an idiot to get lost. I like to look for the chicory with the starburst of cornflower blue blossoms. Folk legend has it that the tips of the leaves will point north.

And down by the beginning of one of the trout streams, where the icy water seems to magically percolate through the gravel bank, there stands an old rotten tree. Gnarled, with a few limbs missing and creating gaping holes in the old trunk, it threatens to fall. It must just face the correct direction, for the reptiles are drawn to its mildly exothermic properties.

In the spring, when the garter snakes come out of their winter hiding places, the males are drawn irresistibly to a lone female - and suddenly there are hundreds of black garter snakes twisting and curling to find that female. The ground seems to be writhing in motion, snakes twisting upon each other and balling into what looks like impossible knots. Sometimes, you see the snakes falling from the rotted holes in the tree trunk. It is a spectacular sight - whether you like black squirming and writhing snakes or not.

One of my favorite trails to run, when I do not have a lot of time, is only about 4 miles long. I park the car about a two-block distance from the intersection, cross the road and pick up the trail about a quarter of a mile away. There is a gap in the tangle of young pines and honeysuckle bushes. I duck and crawl through and pick up this little shortcut of a path made by the rabbits, fox and deer, to catch the trail carved by the Department of Natural Resources. Through this shortcut section, the ground is covered in a thick layer of springy moss that is the color of tarnished gold.

Often, when we have had a refreshing rain, I take the time to examine the moss and am amazed at the detail and organization of these tiny plants. It looks like a very miniature version of the large forest that shades the moss' existence. Even when we have had no rain for a stretch of time, the ground stays moist. I would venture to guess that the underground river must come close to the surface in this area.

The moss must just soak up all the sound because it is always deadly quiet here beneath these pines with the green trunks. Even when I stomp my feet, the sound is gone and I feel as though I have gone slightly deaf. Odd too, how the wind avoids this area. I can hear the wind "shsss" off in the treetops - but here under the perpetually dim light, there is silence.

The most amazing spider webs hang from the trees here. I marvel at a spider who could throw a single thin thread ten feet long and spin a delicate net across the narrow trail to catch....what.

The first time I ran along this trail, not aware of the huge webs, I was the insect that was caught. I ended up with a huge spider web over my face, from my head all the way down to my waist. And for the rest of the four miles I had the creepy tickling sensation that a large spider was crawling about on the back of my neck.

In other areas of the forest, where the pine trees stand tall, the air takes on a quiet misty green color. On a hot summer day, entering these areas is like entering a cool ethereal cave. Spots of sunlight and a flitter of a large swallowtail butterfly draw me on and invite me into a world of peace and harmony.

However, I cannot say the same about the shortcut trail. It is dark and moody, and before I took Pallie running with me, I thought it was just a silly undefined nervousness because I ran the trail alone. But she too, does not like this brief section of the pines. I see her looking over her shoulders with her eyes tensely searching for something. She has no desire to stop or inspect anything until we hop over a particular fallen tree where the sunlight suddenly floods the ground to mark the end of this depressing section.

There is a mile run down the row of pines and suddenly upon climbing a small rise, we stand on the edge of a prairie where a log cabin sits on the crest of a shallow hill. The cabin has been here for over 100 years and the well, now a crumbled pile of decayed wood over a mysterious hole, still echoes the trickling sounds of the artesian water that seeps into it.

Pallie hears things.... and I feel things. I have had occasions where I have felt as though someone poked my shoulder, and swinging my head back quickly, there is a nanosecond of a feeling beside me..........hatred. On the return, Pallie always looks for a way to avoid this last section of the trail - but there is not one. The honeysuckle bushes and thorn bushes grow thick and strangle any route but this. Her intensity returns and she rushes through until she breaks out of the pines to the side of the road. The chicory meet us at the ditch to point:

"Go this way."

On one particular run, we had a late start. So by the time we made our return run, the sun was beginning to hang rather low in the sky. It's what the photographers call the golden hour. Shadows are long and the earth seems to take on a clarity of color that is missing through the day. I was deep in thought and without realizing it, we had stepped past the last patch of sunlight, hopped over the fallen tree and were now in the gloomy stretch of pines.

What a foreboding feeling! Pallie began to whimper and scurried along, casting glances over her shoulder. She wanted out of here and could easily have left me - but she is my soulmate and feels she must stick with me no matter what. Silently she urged me to hurry.

"OK, sweetie, let's sprint." With the last bit of energy, we ran the stretch as fast I could go. We exploded out of the trees, turned right when we hit the road and began slowing down to we walked to the intersection.

But oddly, this time that feeling of hatred clung to me like a cold damp shawl. No matter what I did, I could not shake off the uncomfortable feeling of ill will.

The discomfort felt nearly like fingers over my shoulders, making the hair on the back of my neck stand up. I spun around quickly, almost expecting to see someone right behind me.

Overhead, I heard a small plane drop low in the sky, circle and pass several times, dipping its wings. I waved. It was a familiar plane, and belonged to a friend of mine who flies for one of the major airlines. He had just two years earlier purchased a small plane and for leisure, could be seen flying across the fields that surround our small city. I waved again, and he dipped his wings again. And suddenly the feeling of hatred that had followed me out of the forest vanished.

I thought nothing more of the whole thing until about two weeks later when I ran into Joel in the supermarket. He told me that he had recognized me out on the road near the intersection because I am the only woman in the area that goes running with a Border Collie. Even from the sky, Pallie's large white collar stands out.

"I thought that was you!" he said.

"Yes, that was me - and I recognized your plane. Were you just out for a pleasure cruise in your plane?" I asked.

"No, actually I had a package that I had to deliver for the hospital and was on my way back to the landing strip. Who was that nasty woman running with you?" he asked.

"Nasty woman?"

"Yes, she was running really close behind you. She was waving her fists. Who was that?"

"Joel.... I wasn't running with anybody. It was just me and Pallie."

"Are you sure? I have seen her before, just before you get to that intersection. She steps out of the bushes by the pines...."

The Conspiracy

"Shadow." That might have been a good name for Stevie Ray Dog. Lately the fella has become clingy, and I wonder if it has to do with the series of illnesses/mishaps that my doggies have gone through. Perhaps I have obtained a new status in their eyes:

She Who Heals.

Due to this apparent status change, I have become very valuable to the dogs. They see me as Necessary. Yes, necessary beyond my functions as The Food Provider, The Source of

Entertainment, The Treat Dispenser, Ball and Disc Tosser, Butt Scritcher, Evil One Who Trims Toenails and Executioner of the Forced Baths. And, I heal . . .

I think the dogs had another one of their board meetings while I was out of the house. And, I think it happened shortly after we finished putting up the rest of the fence. Suddenly, with this new bit of freedom, the doggies are acting just a little bit .... hm... different. It must be that independence. They appear to be doing a little more thinking.

"Today, the backyard. Tomorrow...the world."

Oh yes. I saw their black and white bodies moving back and forth on the other side of the fence while we planted a maple tree. Between the narrow slits of the six foot wooden fence, one beady eye after another followed our movements as we walked up and down the fence, laying down black mesh to kill the weeds, and covered it all with cypress mulch. When I stepped back into the backyard again, they all sat down with this suspiciously causal look on their doggie faces. Too nonchalant, me thinks. What could they have been discussing...

"After twelve years, suddenly we have the backyard," says Pallie. "I am suspicious."

"But, wasn't this the goal?" Cap questioned.

"Yes . . . but it took them TWELVE YEARS! Why suddenly after twelve years?" Pallie cocked her head thoughtfully.

"Hmm..." KC sat down and ruminated the idea. He scratched his head lightly with a hind foot.

"I like the fenced yard!" Stevie Ray Dog chimed in.

"Yes . . . so do I," said Pallie thoughtfully. "But there is something about this that worries me."

"Oh? What would that be?" Asked Cap.

All four dogs lay face to face, their front paws nearly touching in sphinx position, and their tails pointed toward the four corners of the world. Stevie twisted his head about to see if the humans were watching. He is the sentry, ya know. He appears to just be following closely all the time – but we suspect he is really on duty. The Tattle Tail.

"Remember how excited the Idiot Dog next door got when he said he was getting a kennel?" Pallie whispered.

"Yes," Cap, KC and Stevie Ray Dog nodded their heads, their ears bobbing slightly.

"Well, Idiot Dog said he'd be outside more often once they put the kennel in - and now look. He's out there: All. Day. Long. And he has that annoying bark going when he tries to tell his humans he wants to come inside to be with them. They ignore him."

"Ahh . . . yesss . . ." the dogs murmured. "Grrr. . ."

"Mom and dad wouldn't do that to us. They are always with us. They said the fenced yard was for us and for our enjoyment," Stevie wrinkled his forehead and his eyebrows twitched up and down as he fixed his BC eye on the others.

"They love us."

"Yes, of course they love us. What's not to love?" Cap stood up and strutted, stretching out his feathery plume of a tail for the others to admire.

"They love us - but we must make sure they don't forget they love us," said wise Pallie. "I am not well, as you know. I feel it is my obligation as leader here to make sure you understand this one very important thing: Never let them forget they love you. You may have to make pests of yourselves to remind them. Think on this, fellow canines. Stevie, I charge you with the mission to keep constant track of mom when she is in the house. I will watch them when we are at work. I won't be here forever to guide you in All Things Human. Let us conspire. . ."

55

I have noticed lately that Stevie Ray Dog is very clingy. He is constantly right behind me, stepping on my heels, leaning against me when I sit down, and breathing his hot breath on my arm.

KC has been poking me in the back of my knee with his wet nose. He smiles at me all the time.

Cap wakes me up every morning by jumping on my bed like a cat and placing a paw lightly on my nose. Every evening, he snuggles up against me for one last tummy rub session, and leaves when he feels me drift off to sleep.

And Pallie, as ever, with her eyes full of conversations, is my constant companion.

I Am Dogless

A silence had fallen over the house. It had been like this for two weeks now, and I had considered its presence for the first time, this evening. I turned my head and listened to it once again. It was loud, clear, and silent.

The silence is not the kind that is void of sound, for sound does happen all about me. I heard the gentle ticking from the clock over the sink, marking each passing second of the silence, and the hum of the refrigerator masks the depths of it. Just beyond the dutch door and attracted to the light, the insects of the night fluttered and bumped against the mullioned window, making their own little ticking sounds. And beyond, the autumn wind blew the first of the yellowed leaves from the large silver maple up against the house. No . . . this is a silence of a different sort.

The lapping at the water bowl unexpectedly interrupted the persiflage of sounds from within the house and out. A curly-coated Border Collie sloshed water about as he drank, careless as an untidy little boy, and dribbled a trail from his chin as he walked toward me. He fixed his eyes upon my face – and suddenly I grasped the substance of the silence.

My foster dog had left me, and I had thought that I would take a short break from fostering. She has a new life filled with new hopes and I will see her again some day, I thought to myself. Her coat will have grown back in and the haunted look that so many rescued dogs have, will be gone from her honey-colored eyes.

Perhaps when she sees me in that distant day, she will recognize me. Her tail will flutter for me as it had so many times while she was here, sitting small and lost against the cupboard doors in the kitchen. But this evening . . .

I am dogless.

Absentmindedly, I ran my fingers through the coat of my blue and white Border Collie – the dog with the arthritis and hip dysplasia. He sat very still, his back to me and with one ear tilted in reverse, listening to my thoughts. He was the first of the needy dogs to come to my home - to sleep in the crate with the pink flowered drape. It is the guest crate - a resting place on a life's journey.

However, this dog had stayed and had taught me that I have room in my home, and within myself, for one more dog. I flattened my hand firmly against his silky coat and made the life and heart lines in my palm become a part of him.

The two dogs settled themselves to the floor under the table and I tucked my toes beneath their warm bodies. Both dogs had been former rescued dogs, and now they were my own. Empathic to my state of mind, commiserating in the sense of loss that had fallen about me, they knew.

I am dogless.

A Perfectly Good Dog

I sat down at my computer and looked at the long list of dogs that were homeless, waiting their fate in one shelter after another, waiting for a rescuer. I looked at the long list of dogs that were still with their owners but no longer wanted, and their fate rested with a rescuer once again. There is only room for one dog here. However, I have chosen to take a short break from fostering.

A photograph came onto the computer screen. It was a bright red fifty-five gallon barrel standing in the corner of a room with a lid over the top. Attached to the lid was a length of tubing connecting it to a tall green cylinder filled with gas.

In my mind's eye, I could see a Border Collie, smart as can be, very aware and knowing, being led to the barrel. He resists with pupils dilated, looses control of his bowels, and his last moments with dignity lost, are filled with screams as the lid drops over his head. A hiss of gas, and then there is silence. An urgent dread suffocates the air from my lungs, and in the quiet atmosphere of my orderly kitchen, I moan to myself.

I am dogless.

A Perfectly Good Dog

Kip

Evening had begun to settle in and once again, I found myself waiting in the parking lot of a restaurant. I checked my watch. Dee would be here soon.

"Good . . . because I'm just a little bit cold."

It was not really that far to the lake. The wind had shifted directions, blowing a cool clammy breeze in from across the water. I sat down at a cold picnic table, opened a book and felt the pages immediately begin to dampen. I ignored all the cars that slowly crawled into parking spots. Each driver turned a curious eye toward me, wondering why anyone would be sitting here, outside in the dimming light, reading a book at this time of the evening when it was the dinner hour for most folks.

"Grace?"

I looked up to see a woman standing on the other side of the narrow parking lot. She had beautiful thick dark hair pulled back away from her pretty face. She smiled warmly and I felt as though I had known her for a long time. There had been a picnic that day. Dee looked tired but content. Her white shirt held memories in the shape of dusty paw prints, and I decided that I should not keep her too long. I was most certain she was tired and just wanted to get home.

Dee opened the back door of her vehicle and a small classic patterned Border Collie lightly dropped to the ground. Ah. So, this was Kip. His coat, ruffled in all directions, looked as though someone had petted his body without concern for what he might look like afterward. His ears were spread wide and revealed his uncertainty. He looked so tiny and fragile with slender legs.

Kip turned his face toward me and fixed the most intense stare upon me. He had spooky eyes; dark gold in color with tight black pupils. He stood motionless and studied me. I thought: "this must be one of the reasons why Kip had not been adopted yet. His eyes would frighten most people who are not familiar with the Border Collie "eye."

I walked toward him and his ears folded neatly behind his head. His tail began to wag slowly and he stepped up to greet me. Quietly and calmly, he stretched his head forward and placed it in the palm of my hand. Even in the fading light, I could see his coat was dry and thin. I ran a long stroke down the length of his body and felt bone after bone. The vertebrae along his spine felt like a row of robin eggs, and the bones of his pelvis jutted out, further stating he was too thin. Then he smiled at me and gently leaned against my legs.

I clipped my leash to his collar, and he understood that he was leaving Dee. A moment of hesitation flashed across his delicate face, and he quickly trotted over to Dee for confirmation that it was indeed ok to be handed off to a complete stranger.

"Kip, let's go." With one last backward glance at Dee, Kip followed me to my jeep and quickly hopped inside without hesitation.

He settled himself quietly and I did not hear a peep from him the entire journey home.

September 16

Donning a pair of gold-rimmed reading glasses, I settled myself at the kitchen table with a sheaf of papers in hand. They were Kip's vet records:

It was a warm and sunny day. The rescuers had set up their booth at the park and were enjoying the activities of the "Dog Day." There were numerous breeds in attendance, and the rescuers quietly commented on the dogs as they walked by. Eventually a man approached them walking two very large and beautiful dogs of a northern breed, and with him, in tow, was a slender wisp of a Border Collie. He appeared to be young dog with a high tuck to his lean body. Even from a distance, the rescuers could tell that this dog was too thin. The man stopped to chat and brought forward the Border Collie.

The rescuers asked the man what he had been feeding the dogs and why this Border Collie was so very thin, whereupon the man explained that his sister had rescued this dog a year ago, and ever since, she had been keeping him inside a corn crib.

One of the rescuers reached forward and the skinny Border Collie walked into her arms, sensing the spirit of love that had begun radiating off her and toward him. He was happy for the attention, and soon he had crawled into her lap. Up close, he was a rack of bones, his hips protruding sharply. The rescuer felt a large lump rising into her throat and soon tears began.

"It looks like this bothers you," said the man.

"Yes, it always does," Amy replied. She felt she could not endure this any longer and got up to leave while angry feelings flooded over her. The man, sensing the discussion had probably ended, began to pull the skinny Border Collie out of her lap, and it became quite apparent that the Border Collie was terrified of leaving. He began shaking horribly. He did not want to go with the man.

"I'll take him," said another one of the rescuers, without hesitation. She already had a house full of dogs - but here was this one, standing there before her, doing his best to plead for help. The man just happened to have the dog's vet papers with him, and he signed over ownership to the Rescue.

Kip had been in Rescue for six months and had put on very little weight. In fact, at the age of four months, he had weighed twenty pounds. He was now four-years old, had come into rescue weighing twenty-two pounds, and gained an additional seven pounds due to the supreme efforts of his previous foster mom.

Kip had been adopted once, but was returned. He had lost weight again. His previous foster mom had written saying how alarmed she was by his weight loss and was once again struggling to get him to eat.

I studied Kip's very skinny little frame and his dry coat. After this length of time in rescue, why was he still looking so weedy? The thin body could be attributed to the mentality of the dog, which we called "chronically starved." But the dry coat? Could there possible other reasons for his thinness and the coat? I could envision him a year from now with his wavy coat full and thick. Interestingly, even his whiskers were curly.

Several thoughts went through my mind: intestinal worms, liver problems, systemic yeast infection, and hypothyroidism. Although a blood panel had been run a year ago, and some of the values were low normal, I decided it was time to run another check and deworm him once again. The hypothyroidism seemed a far stretch since most dogs with this condition are overweight – but I did foster a dog at one time that was very thin and had a low thyroid score . . .

Kip settled himself in the floral-patterned snuggler I had put under the kitchen table. His records indicated that he would hide away in his crate all day if he was not encouraged to come out or if the door was not closed to prevent him from entering the crate. He looked up at me with eyes full of doubts – yet he did not seem to lack confidence. He just was not sure what was going on, and he did not know what was expected of him. The snuggler, out there in the kitchen, was a good compromise, and he latched onto it most happily. He was in the open but felt he was tucked away at the same time.

Dave and I stood leaning against the kitchen counter, discussing Kip – and he obviously knew we were talking about him. He followed our voices back and forth like a spectator at a tennis match. Tomorrow blood would be drawn to compare the bloodwork from a year ago.

September 17

The results of Kip's blood work came back. It looked better than it had a year ago, and his thyroid test was normal. I was very happy to see this. I had now ruled out physical reasons for Kip's extreme thinness; it was time to seriously consider the reason as being a psychological one. Kip had the mindset of the chronically starved dog. I could put my thumbs and middle fingers together to form a complete circle around Kip's loin – and my hands are not very big.

I went back to the records and studied the variety of efforts the others had tried to encourage Kip to eat. He had been given Satin Balls, which are high in calories; he had been fed in his crate to avoid the sense of competition. He had been fed several smaller meals throughout the day. He had been fed one meal in the evening. He had been fed a variety of enticing foods with his kibble. He had been fed just dry kibble. He had been given warm liquid in his kibble. And his weight had not changed.

Since Kip would spend his day in his crate if allowed, I decided that feeding him in the crate would only encourage this behavior. At first, I tried feeding him in the bathroom with the doors closed so he could have privacy. This did not work. Next, I fed him in the kitchen and let the sense of competition for food compel him to eat. He watched the other Border Collies nervously - who completely ignored him - and let out a nervous "Oooo!" as his eyes darted back and forth from one dog to another. They continued to ignore him and calmly left the kitchen once their bowls were empty, as though he did not exist. Kip looked greatly relieved and ate a little better.

Kip's records indicated that he had the beginnings of some mineralization in his neck. Perhaps he had just a bit of discomfort in his neck when he lowered his head to the floor. I put his food bowl on a small bucket, which lifted the bowl a foot off the floor. He was delighted with this and began to eat a little more.

I added 2000 mgs of Salmon oil to each feeding (two meals per day) gave him vitamin B complex, vitamin E, Seameal, and Alpha-

Lipoic acid. His meal was now a heaping ladle of homemade beef, vegetable, noodle, barley, and rice soup, an egg, a cup of his kibble, and a dollop of plain yogurt. Then I added a new command to his list of known commands.

"Kip: eat."

At the end of a week, he had finally managed to gain one pound.

September 21

Autumn settled in subtly. The summer had been painfully dry – so dry that many farmers had plowed under their crops or picked them early. The survivors were the broad fields of soybeans, which had now turned into tight rows, like a scrub brush, of bristling golds and caramel. Patches of soy on the sides of steeper hills still held their leaves and struggled to maintain a lime green.

Off in the distance, the popping sounds of gunfire announced the flight of the Canadian Geese, headed out to the dwindling cornfields, still heavy with dew, for an early morning breakfast. Did Kip remember the cornfields and the corncrib where he had spent so many hours alone and forgotten?

This morning I took Kip for a hike out in the state forest. We stood on the deck and waited for a couple of friends to arrive. Neither had met Kip yet and I was curious to see what kind of reaction they would have when they met him – and how Kip would react to meeting complete strangers. His previous foster homes said he was lacking confidence, but I had not observed that from him. My impression was that he was introspective upon meeting new people and situations. He would take a minute to consider everything – and then step forward.

Sure enough. Kip stood back and watched my four Border Collies squirm and wiggle about the visitors, joyously happy. His tail was not tucked beneath him, nor were his ears folded back nervously. He was curious and waited to be invited for a proper greeting.

Both women were immediately overcome with sympathy at the sight of him: so skinny, so small and fragile in appearance. He had melted their hearts. Neither thought his dark gold eyes to be intimidating. Both agreed that all it would take an adopter was just a few minutes with him to see what a precious little fella he is. Kip quickly made friends with them and cuddled up against them for a little extra petting.

The weather was glorious. We hiked an "Out & Back" trail that climbed over a lengthy esker, wound its way through long rows of pines, and meandered over a jumble of erratics in the midst of the deciduous forest. The effects of the long summer drought and the cool nights had thinned the leaves from the trees. It was already possible to look back through the forest to the undulating hills normally hidden in thick vegetation.

Kip was utterly delighted to be out in the wilds. He kept his nose busy, sniffing the scent of animals that had long ago passed this way. Soon the chittering sounds of chipmunks became mesmerizing, and his ears popped up like radarscopes to zero in on them. By the end of two hours, fatigue settled in, and we headed back home. All during the hike, I found myself worrying about his weight.

"He's going to burn some of those calories I worked so hard to put on him . . ."

Upon returning home, he had a long drink of water, ate nearly two cups of a thick stew mixed with kibble, then threw himself into his snuggler under the kitchen table, then slept the rest of the afternoon with a little smile on his face.

The weekly Weigh In:

I hooked the black frayed leash to Kip's collar – the same leash so recently worn by beautiful little Ayla. She was now happily ensconced in her new home and once again, the frayed edges of my heart reminded me of how much I missed her. I thought it very likely that Kip would have the same effect when he eventually left my care.

Kip rides beautifully in the car. The moment I opened the door, he hopped in and settled quietly inside. I would have expected that all the transfers and life changes he had gone through would have made him suspicious of getting into a vehicle. Not so. He was glad to go anywhere with me.

Today, the trip was to the Whitewater Veterinary Hospital. I wanted to weigh him since it had been a week, and he had been eating his food with little hesitation. Kip floated out of the jeep and checked out his new surroundings. His nose picked up a multitude of scents in the bushes around the vet clinic. (I have always marveled that these bushes managed to be alive and green with all the "watering" they got).

"Hi Grace!" the vet techs called out.

"I just want to weigh Kip again, ok?"

"Sure."

"Kip, come. He trotted over to the scale.

"Kip, stand." Like the very obedient dog that he is, Kip stood perfectly still on the scale. Last week he had weighed 30.5 pounds. I held my breath:

"30.6 pounds. Oh Kip... I don't believe it. You've only gained one ounce the whole week!" He wagged his tail happily at me.

September 28

Kip has become a talker: all kinds of vocalizations to express his range of moods and needs. I read somewhere that the intelligent dog speaks with more vocalizations than a dog of lesser intelligence. So there you have it: living proof in the form of a skinny little Border Collie. If only he could say all those things in English...

Earlier in the week, I wiggled my bare feet under his body, and he looked up at me as though to say,

"Are we sharing the snuggler?" Then he plopped his slender paw over my ankle and laid his chin down on my toes.

A few moments later, I began singing softly to myself. Kip had been sleeping – but his eyes popped open wide and he tipped his head sideways with his ears spread out. I'm wasn't sure if he hadn't been sung to before, if he didn't like my song selection – or maybe he didn't like me trying to sing with a cold. Kip was soon crooning along with me. He crawled up into my lap and laid his chin on my collarbone.

Ever since, I have been singing to him each evening. He now lays on my feet and stares up at me as though he understands the words to the song. When I finish, he nuzzles his head into my hands with a happy smile on his delicate face.

The weekly Weigh-In

Like a very good boy, Kip scurried over to the scale and laid down on it.

"Woo Hoo! Kip! 31.4 pounds, Kip! This is the most you have ever weighed." I smiled broadly at him and he looked very pleased with himself.

October 4

Kip has grown quite accustomed to his quiet days here with me. The routine is predictable and gives him the "sense of security" that seems to scuttle away from him at the most unexpected moments.

Today, I threw him a curve ball. I took him to work with me in the afternoon. We had gone for a three-mile walk, first stopping to say "hi" to the nice man at the gas station. Jerry loves dogs. He will drop to his knees on the pavement and call to the dogs with his arms spread wide.

"Well git over here. Git over here."

The Border Collies love to get their backs scratched, and Cap will lean most happily into Jerry, trying to gather up as much of Jerry's attention as possible. Kip will sit back politely and wait his turn.

"Come here, Mr. Skinny Bones," Jerry held his hands out calmly and coaxed Kip to him. Just what Kip was waiting for: the invitation. Quietly and tentatively, Kip approached Jerry and sat down very sweetly before him.

With a sadly tranquil expression, Jerry tenderly ran his large hand over tiny little Kip's frame. His face described the emotion

71

buried in his chest, as he looks at Kip. I watched him swallow hard. Such a big softie, that Jerry.

"Are you being a good boy? Cleaning your plate like you're supposed to?" Kip snuggled closer to Jerry and gave him a wag of his tail.

After the walk, I opened the jeep's door and Kip popped right in, settling himself in the back without a thought as to where I might be taking him. He trotted down the sidewalk with me, shooting quick glances at me.

"I've never been here before. Where are you taking me?" Kip's step became a bit more tentative. He scrambled inside the building, unsure of himself until Pallie and KC walked up to greet him. His confidence returned… and then wavered.

"This is a store, Kip. It's a dog friendly place."

I encouraged Kip to greet a few customers, and he did quite well. However, after the three customers, he was obviously becoming stressed. I sat on the floor with him and he snuggled tight against me with his front paws on my lap. He tucked head into my sweatshirt and buried his face.

"Kip, look at me," I whispered, lifting his head.

His eyes were full of uncertainty and his lower jaw quivered in a rapid staccato. He hid his head into my sweatshirt again. I took him back up to the office where a fleece snuggler lay tucked under the desk, and Kip ran to it. It became his island of safety. He buried himself in the snuggler and slept quietly for the remaining three hours. Poor baby.

The Weigh-In Weekly

"Oh Kip! You weigh 31.5 pounds!" (Yes, I do believe his ribs are every so slightly filling in. Two weeks to gain one ounce).

Kip just loves to go for walks. The moment he sees his blue harness, he will scurry over and sit down ever so politely in front of me. He has begun to talk about his excitement too – little growly sounds. His eyes are bright with excitement that runs all the way down to the white tip of his tail.

Slowly, I lowered the harness over his head. One ear tipped backward, as he waited to be fitted, listening to the "Click" that tells him he is all set to go. Light as a feather, he bounced to his feet.

Sam and Marie arrived with Gil the Yellow Lab. We headed off to the state forest for a long hike. Kip was extremely excited upon seeing Gil again. He immediately began "talking" up a storm. Obviously to Kip, the sight of Gil means we are going hiking. We parked in the small gravel lot and climbed the stony path that wound its way to the top of Star Hill. A split rail fence and bench marked the top of the climb, and we took a quick breather.

The wind ruffled past the elms and oak trees, knocking off a flurry of leaves. We stood for a moment and watched them swirl through the air high above us as though an enormous invisible hand had stirred them. Kip was anxious to explore the other side of Star Hill, and we scrambled down the long decent strewn with rocks. Gill the Lab - whose body weight is easily two and a half times Kip's - was ahead and it was most obvious to Kip that the puppy was not being properly managed. We found it best to keep these two dogs as close together as possible.

There was a Hiking Event going on and we passed quite a few people. Everyone stopped to greet the dogs. Kip snuggled right up to them all. Funny how one week he was so very shy and the next he is bursting with confidence.

October 20

The Weekly Weigh-In

By now, Kip has learned the routine and getting on the scale is a piece of cake. I called him over and he scurried over, sat his skinny little butt down and smiled at me, knowing that he had done exactly what was expected of him.

"Kip! A new record for you! Congratulations, sweetie. Shake, Kip." He placed a slender paw in my hand. I am sure he must have thought I was so easy to please. All he had to do was sit down on that low, flat black mat in the corner of the vet clinic and I would be suddenly very pleased with him. Humans: they are soo easy.

Kip now weighs 32 pounds. About another five pounds and he will be a Thin Dog. The additional weight seems to have had other effects upon him as well. Kip is livelier now. Every morning he scurries out of his crate and follows me about the house. He knows not to jump up in my face - but if I turn my back, I can feel him bounce off my hips. When I turn around, he begins the "Happy Dance" and talks away to me, telling me how very happy he is that morning has arrived and we will be together again. He will jump up in the air and leap backward, wiggling. When his front feet meet the floor, he does a tap dance and the hind end of him does the hoochy koochy.

Kip has been eating better. The secret has been the tablespoon of melted butter poured over his meal. I've tried just setting his bowl down without adding the butter - but he'll walk up to the bowl, sticking his nose in and will give it a sniff of inspection. Then he will look at me calculatingly:

"Excuse me. You've forgotten my butter."

This afternoon we took a five-mile walk about town. It was an unusually warm day - probably one of the last ones of the year. The maple trees are shedding their leaves in lovely jewel tones of golds and coppers. Everywhere piles of leaves lay mounded on front lawns. One house had a long pile with a pair of stuffed jeans and cowboy boots sticking out of the end of the leaf pile. Homes have been decorated with large orange pumpkins and wispy strands of fiberglass "spider webs." At first Kip regarded these lawn ornaments with deep suspicion - but squirrels have been so busy chasing about, he has forgotten to notice them and has been leaping up at the base of the trees, intend on those "tree sheep."

The leaves of autumn tumbled about us, driven by the light breeze. I could imagine Kip as a young pup, and I would not doubt that he would have pounced on them with delight, pinning them to the ground to control their movement. With his ears held high and his eyes bright, Kip trotted along, leaving messages for all the other dogs to read:

Kip was Here
This is My Tree
Read This and Weep

October 27

The Weekly Weigh-In

"Kip..." (sigh) "Not an ounce. You haven't put on so much as an ounce this whole week. Where are you putting that food I've been giving you? What. Not enough butter, you say? Do you realize I now buy three pounds a week instead of one?"

Kip crawled up into my lap and laid his head on my chest, happy to be so near me. I had such high hopes for some weight gain this week. Kip has been eating so good. I think we are finally over the hump and he is just about over his psychological need to save a little bit of food back in case I decide to starve him. He has been cleaning his bowl up ever so nicely - except he still thinks he needs to keep just a little bit back. Just in case.

He really does want to clean his food bowl out but cannot quite bring himself to do it. It is comical to see what he leaves behind, and I have begun to think that he can count to four.

This week, the sweetest little Border Collie to ever walk the face of the planet, Ayla, is here while her new mom is away on vacation. To my surprise, her presence has presented a new attitude from Kip. He's jealous! He not thrilled about sharing his favorite person and has actually gotten a little pushy at times. I have to smile.

Kip grumbled to himself, squeezed into my lap to gather me all to himself, and scowled at Ayla. She, on the other hand, is demure, polite and such a love. The two together are just darling, each snuggling up to me for loving. They are so different from each other, and both are so precious. Of the two, Kip has the most personality. He is just marvelous in his ability to express himself.

November 3

Although at times, very subtle and waning, Kip's courage has been gradually improving. His furtive glances when we are out for our daily walks have completely vanished. A vigorous, excited pulling dog now replaces that. Yes! He now pulls on his leash! I never thought I would see the day when that happened. He is animated, leaping about and barking in Cap's face.

"Let's play! You be the sheep and I'll herd you!"

This morning we woke to thunder storms and a gray atmosphere. The house was so dark; I overslept by half an hour. My beautiful alpha female, Pallie, was anxious for me to get up. She pawed my side of the bed and tapped impatiently at her wristwatch.

"Mom, it's time to get up. You have to take me out. Ok... you have to take those other dogs out too – but me, I am most important here. Get up, mom!"

(All right, so she doesn't really wear a wristwatch. However, she is convinced she can tell time better than I can. She does know left/right better that I do...which makes me feel really stupid at times... We are still negotiating on the wristwatch thing).

Ayla has returned home now, and we are back down to only five Border Collies. For some odd reason, the house seems somewhat

77

lonely without her. I opened the backdoor and picked up the tie-out. Five Border Collies lowered their heads and stood back with their noses wiggling side to side as they sniff the pouring rain out there on the deck. None of them wanted to step outside.

"Well?" I said.

They all backed up, and Kip scurried under the kitchen table to his Snuggler Island – the haven in the storm of life. He averted his face, thinking if he did not look at me, I would not see him.

"Listen," I scowled at the five. "You have relatives out there in Wales, who roam the hills up and down, herding up the sheep and covering as much as a hundred miles a day during the six weeks of lambing season. And they get up the next morning to do it again. Do you think they worry about a little downpour of rain? No."

Five doggie faces gazed past me, all of them suddenly having gone deaf. I called Kip to me and he scurried over, being the very obedient little fella that he is.

"Now pay attention, doggies. See how brave Kip is? A little rain isn't going to melt him away – and it won't hurt you either. All you have to do is go out there, potty, and you can come back inside."

Their faces lit up.

"Ohhh…. We thought you wanted us to round up sheep out in the rain."

The Weekly Weigh-In

Yes! A new record! Kip now weighs 32.6 pounds. I had been worried that he had lost a little bit of weight since his appetite had gone somewhat flat during the past two days. He has been rather consistent about eating pretty well – and then losing interest after about three weeks.

A food change might be in order again. I had noticed his searching for something specific to eat when the other dogs were content to eat the couch grass. Kip is looking for some kind of plant that has a round leaf. I don't what that plant is or what it is that he thinks he needs. Therefore, I got a bottle of liquid multiple vitamins. I will begin adding that to his food again to see if it makes a different in his appetite.

November 10

The Weekly Weigh-In

Kip walked into the vet clinic with an air of nonchalance. Without any coaching, he trotted over to the flat black mat in the corner and immediately settled himself down on the scale. Flipping his head up toward me, he jiggled his tail. Already he was expecting big praise from me.

I crossed my fingers and glanced up at the reading on the scale while holding my breath.

"Kip! 32.8 pounds! You've gained again. I am so proud you!" I gathered him up into my arms and gently hugged him. He beamed at me and gave me light kisses on the chin.

Behind the receptionist's desk sat Patty (who has been watching these weekly weigh-ins) and Bonnie (who has never seen them).

79

"Yeah Kip!!" Patty cheered. Two thumbs up and a big smile from her – while Bonnie looked at us as if we were daft.

"32.6 last week and 32.8 this week? And you think that's great?!" Bonnie shook her head and took the pencil from behind her ear to record his weight.

Kip made his feelings known to Bonnie by sitting down with his back to her. Bonnie's mouth formed a circle and her neck craned forward as she studies his delicate little frame.

"Oh my gosh. Is he skinny," she muttered and shook her head. "He's got that hourglass figure that woman would die for. He's so narrow!"

"Yeah well... his whole chest is filled with a great big heart. Isn't that right, Kip. Let's go, sweetie. You are such a good boy." Kip trotted out the door and hopped into the jeep.

The weather had turned rather cold this week, with temperatures down in the 20's during our morning walks. Crisp, cold air blew all the remaining leaves off the big maple tree in the front yard. They lay like a bright gold halo around the base of the tree: a tangible patch of sunlight.

Kip was cold. Shy dogs often "blow their coats" when they come into rescue. Stress from the change in environment, the change in diet, household members, routine, and learning a new place will cause an amazing amount of shedding. Dry, brittle fur had been falling off Kip for the first month. It was now thin with very little undercoat, and Kip began shivering within ten minutes. He was going to need a little bit of help until his coat grew back in again. This winter, he was going to be cold without the undercoat and without body fat.

I brought out a T-shirt and put it on him backward, so that the front was now over his back. Then I cut a long slit in the shirt from the hem to mid chest on his under side, and crossed the ends of the slit, making them meet again on top of his back. There was just enough fabric to tie the ends together. The sleeves were too long. I cut them off. Kip's chest and back were now covered while his hind end was free to relieve himself when he needed to without getting his shirt wet.

The most interesting thing about wrapping Kip like this is that it does more than just keep him warm. I have used the T-shirt wrap to prevent a dog from licking incisions as well. However, for the shy dog, there is one extra benefit of the T-shirt wrap: it helps build confidence. The shirt acts kind of like a hug and helps prevent that feeling that he is flying out in every direction.

Contained and warm, Kip's attitude was joyously happy. He danced out the door doing the Highland Fling while yodeling his delight.

This evening I fed him his meal while he wore his shirt – and he ate every bit.

November 15

I did something that I have never done before: I called an Animal Communicator. Skeptical but curious, I just had to know if this could be for real. On the recommendation from two of my friends, Renee and Jayne, I gave Doris a call. Besides, this might be fun if not anything else.

Doris started by making contact with Kip, who was nestled in his snuggler under the kitchen table. I was standing in the dining room with my cell phone. There was a long pause as Doris attempted to make contact with Kip. Suddenly he came scurrying into the dining room and laid down about six feet away looking like a little sphinx. I sat down on the floor but he did not come to me. His ears were up and he had a serious expression on his face. He looked as though he was listening to someone - and he knew it was not I. He was amazingly calm and very still. Ordinarily he would have been in my lap - but not this time.

Doris said that Kip has a tiny stomach and he cannot eat very much at one time. She said he is small and very narrow. When outside he is been looking for something to eat and cannot find it. He told her it was a mint plant. Yes, that fits. I have noticed him searching for a round leaf plant, tasting many and spitting them all out. I have not taken him anywhere that the mint grows. Tomorrow morning, I am going to test this and see if it truly is mint that he has been looking for. She said Kip says his tummy feels better after a little bit of mint leaf. (She also suggested giving him a tablespoon of beer within an hour of his meal, and he would eat better).

Kip told Doris that he worries about food; that it would not always be there and he must save some, if he could. She told him he did not need to worry about food. It will always be there for him. He also told her that he is somewhat shy and that he will always be this way. He knows that I know this, and he hopes that I will understand it will always be this way.

I told Doris to tell Kip that I love him very much. There was a pause as she told him, and then Kip came over to me and sat down in front of me. He folded his ears back and gave me a big smile. He put his paw on my forearm, and then gave me a kiss on the chin. I asked Doris to tell Kip that he was not staying here with me forever. Kip got nervous and crawled into my lap.

Doris told Kip that I was his grandmother and his new mom is coming to get him tomorrow, and that she loves him very much already. He will have a sister. (Glory is a red/white BC). Kip said he would like that, having a sister. He got off my lap and put his paw back on my forearm. He smiled demurely and told her that he was nervous but was kind of looking forward to meeting his new mom.

Then he told her I have been grandmother to many dogs. I asked Doris to tell Kip that I will miss him very much. Kip got all upset and crawled into my lap again, trembling slightly. Then I told him even if I never get to see him again, I will always keep track of him and if he ever has to, he will come back to me. I will always be here for him.

Doris said his tummy just relaxed, and at the same moment, he crawled off my lap again and placed his paw on my arm with a big smile on his face, pulling my arm toward him. He looked up at me and she said he said thank you - at the same moment he was doing this.

"Oh," Doris said, "Kip wants to know if he can take his woobie with him."

I smiled. He had arrived with two blankets that I had been calling his woobies. He had smiled big the moment I had taken them out of the bag and placed them in his crate on his first night here. I had not said anything to anyone about his woobies. Kip likes arranging them in his crate every night.

I hung up the phone and Kip scurried back to his snuggler. Usually when I sit down at the table, he immediately crawls up into my lap. Tonight, he does not seem to need to do this. And he has been very calm.

This morning Kiip was interestingly different. He was not his usually loud and happy self, bouncing off me and trying to hop into my lap the moment I sat down. I really do think the talk with the animal communicator made a difference. Kip was quiet this morning and very calm. He ate nearly all of his meal and settled into his snuggler.

Karin and Steve arrived at 9:00, and Kip walked up to Karin when she called him. He smiled for her and pushed his chest into her

83

hands. I don't think there was any hesitation about it either. Karin got a new black harness for Kip and the moment it came out of the bag, Kip was right there with a smile.

Karin and Steve, Kip, Cap and Pallie went out for a long walk so they could see how joyously happy Kip gets when he is outside. The day was ominous with rain, and a very fine mist hung in the air. Damp and somewhat cold, the chill sank deeply into the core of me. A warmth was leaving me soon – that skinny little Border Collie who desperately had clung to a lonely life. His warmth and tender little ways would soon be miles and miles from me. I must smile and be happy for Kip.

They put him on a long flexi and he obeyed their every command. He is such a good little dog. They brought along a video camera to film their meeting with Kip, and their daughter called three times. What nice people they are. I had a very good feeling about them and knew in my heart that Kip would be happy here.

When it came near time for them to leave, Kip left his snuggler in the kitchen and came into the dining room to my chair. He wrapped his front paws around my hips and tucked his face under my arm, then turned his head the other direction and laid his ear against my heart. It was a long and very sweet embrace. He knew.

He gazed into my face so solemnly, and once again tucked his face under my arm. I gave him his last back massage and rubbed the inside of his ears the way he likes them rubbed. I gave him a kiss on the top of his head, and he stared at me for a moment.

We went back into the kitchen while Karin and Steve put their jackets and shoes back on. Kip came over and sat down in front on me again. A look of excitement, mixed with apprehensions, filled his gentle face. He needed one more moment of reassurance from me. I got on the floor with him and massaged the tension from his chest, and gave him one more kiss.

"Kip, I love you. Be a very good boy and make me proud of you. I'll always be here Kip. Don't forget me." He smiled at me and seemed ready to go.

I walked out to the car with them, and skinny little Kip looked ever so small and delicate. Briefly, I thought:

"He's too little to send out into such a big world..."

Suddenly, like a drowning person seeing a lifetime of memories flash by, I saw all the wonderful Border Collies that had been in my care, and I remembered each adoption day. Each one had been a mixture of happiness filled with a great amount of selfish sorrow. I had let another wonderful little soul leave my home, and I felt that stabbing pain with each heartbeat... a bleeding within. My little foster dog was gone again.

Keeping the foster dog is not my purpose here. My purpose is to rescue the Border Collie in need. Sometimes the dog is a stray whose time is up at the shelter. Other times, it is a family that cannot or will not keep their dog for one reason or another.

A needy Border Collie will spend time with me to learn basic manners. I house train and crate train the dog if it has not been done. All vaccinations are brought up to day, a fecal check and heartworm check is done, and the dog is microchipped.

Often the dog has health issues of one sort or another. There have been blind dogs and deaf dogs that have been my "guest." There have been dogs recovering from heartworm disease, kennel cough, infections, broken bones, in need of dental work, and seriously ill from intestinal worms. Most seriously, I have cared for dogs who have lost the people they love. Heartsick, feeling lost and alone, and unable to communicate with the humans around them, they have found a warm and safe haven here with me.

It is always a heartwarming day when my foster dog realizes I am the person who understands his needs. The foster dog is happy to I am a person who will set down boundaries that are clear. With boundaries, the foster dog knows what is acceptable and what is not. That knowledge also brings the comfort of knowing, he is safe within those boundaries.

I remember a deaf Border Collie who came to me for foster care. She lost her home because she liked to chase the cars along the road and herd the horses. The owners, afraid there would come a day when a spooked horse would drop its rider, decided it was best for the dog to be rehomed.

She did not understand the concept that humans can talk to dogs. Not ever having heard sound, I began to teach her American Sign Language. It was a difficult thing to teach her the abstract concept of a word belonging to an object. Much more difficult was teaching her commands.

One day, she sat in the living room while the sun spread across the floor to warm her white coat. I pointed to a ball and made the hand sign for ball. She cocked her head, looked at me and then at the ball. I pointed once again and made the hand sign, then picked up the ball.

Suddenly her face exploded into a big smile and her tail wagged furiously. She finally understood. With great joy, she sprang to her feet and rushed over to another toy, poked it with her nose, and then looked up at me expectantly. I made the hand sign for the toy, and she was delighted.

For the next half hour, she danced about the house, poking objects with her nose, then looking up at me. What a happy day that was for both of us.

It usually takes a very well adjusted rescued Border Collie about month to recover from the transitions between losing his home, going to foster care, and then on to a new home.

Border Collies who have serious health issues or have not had the benefit of a good foundation will take many months to learn and recover. The longer they stay with me, the harder it is to let them go.

The tail, which had been stuck tightly to the dog's tummy, slowly relaxes and I see that tail wag. Soon, the little "hook" on the end of the tail appears, and I know it is time for my foster dog to leave my care.

Kip is gone from my care now. There will be no more "popcorn kisses" and no more of Kip's hoochy koochy dancing around my feet. Kip hopped right into their car and snuggled himself into the quilt that covered the seat – as though he belonged there. Karin got in the back with him for the long ride home, intent on cuddling and bonding with him the whole way home. He smiled at her as she settled in beside him.

There are no more "Kip smiles" for me now either. They belong to another. Sigh...my purpose for being in Kip's life is completed.

I turned slowly back to the house, and paused to have a few quiet moments to myself. I sat down on the deck, tucking my feet beneath me, and folded my arms tight about me. In my mind, I saw the

Path of Life. Many of these little paths have crossed mine. At times, they have run parallel to mine before they drifted off in another direction.

A little dog track, no wider than Kip's narrow little body, joined my path for such a short time, and we climbed the gentle slopes and dips together. He trotted along happily beside me, reluctant at times to follow me.

"This way, Kip! Your path is my path for a while. Do not worry, little one. I have your leash firmly in my hand, and as long as you walk beside me through this portion of your Path, you are safe. Take courage. Smile for me, little Kip. Be brave – and if you cannot find it within yourself to be brave, then lean on me and I will be your courage for now. This way, little Kip."

I closed my eyes and whisked away the moisture that slid down my cheek. In my mind, I heard the hum of life along The Path. Here, it sang quietly like the flutter of wings and the hum of the honeybee. Kip's Path and mine have come to the wide-open meadow. I stopped to gaze across the fields of green and the wild flowers.

Squinting, and hoping to catch a glimpse of what lies ahead, I see Kip's narrow little Path separate from mine to join another. It pushed through the brightly colored meadow blossoms, up the hill and disappeared over the crest. I whispered into the wind:

"Good-bye, little Kip. Perhaps we will meet again. I love you Kip."

The Blue Jacket

The first cool days of autumn had arrived. I stood on the sidewalk for a moment, watched a flurry of dry silver maple leaves swirl about me, and listened to the sound. The leaves dashed themselves to the pavement before they raced down the street, chattering madly to themselves. Beautiful colors were coming alive all around me; deep rust on the tops of the sumac bushes, rich plum colors, sparkling greens and sallow yellows in the cattails and piercing oranges and gold high in the trees above. The earth smelled of damp sod, mist and musky molds.

There was a tug on my wrist from the leashes attached to the three Border Collies. It was morning and there were things to sniff, messages to leave on the battered old railing that guarded the spillway, and squirrels to harass.

They were eager to be about their business, and if I was going to come along with them, then I must pick up my pace. Heavily bedecked in argent droplets, bright as mercury, the couch grass had already turned my shoes soggy. I ducked beneath the silver strands of spider webs that floated on the light breeze, and we headed down toward the lake.

It was very early. It was so early that I was the only human in the world to be out and about. I smiled to myself and realized that if it were not for these lovely Border Collies who insisted on being outside so early, I would still be in bed, sound asleep, and missing the beauty of the early morning.

A light mist began to fall, dampening the sounds and creating a nether world affect. Today, I decided, we would walk through the cemetery. It had been a month since we had strolled through the tall wrought iron gates and climbed the sinewy esker that edged the lake.

On a wet morning such as this, there would be no one in the cemetery – not a living soul, so to speak. Perhaps we would encounter the ghost of Mary Worth again. Dressed in a long dark coat with a bustle in the back, and her dark hair pulled up high above her tall collar, Pallie and I had come upon her twice before as she floated up the hill to the mausoleum.

I truly missed walking through the cemetery. However, a decree was passed by the Cemetery Committee, which forbade dogs, bicycles, and anglers from enjoying the quiet solitude here down by the lake and amidst the ancient gravestones. Over at the far end of the cemetery, my dear friend Bill who had died of cancer lay beneath a black granite marker.

"Come visit me, Grace. Everyone else will eventually forget about me.... but I have the feeling that you will always remember me." His eyes had been sunken deep within his skull from his suffering. His sentences came through in shallow puffs while the oxygen filtered into his agonized lungs. His lovely blue eyes were now dark and oddly colorless, reflecting only his torturous pain.

"I don't mind dying – it is the process of dying, and leaving my wife and three little girls behind that I mind so terribly. I have asked God many times: 'Why?' He does not answer me . . ."

"I don't know, Bill. I don't know. . ."

I kept my promise to him for years, walking my Border Collies through the cemetery and acknowledging his existence, his love and remembering his dreams and hopes for his life. However, the Cemetery Committee had decreed that Bill was dead - and the living, which still breathed life, hope, love and dreams - should go elsewhere to enjoy those things Bill wanted to do. Let the dead remain quiet and be all but forgotten. It was the respectful thing to do, they said.

Bill would not have wanted that: to be so respectfully left alone. I remembered him as a "people person" with a big hearty laugh. I sighed to myself - and decided that since I was the only person in the world to be awake and out for a morning walk, we would walk the narrow paths that wound through the cemetery, and visit Bill again.

From the top of the esker, the sun broke through the old Norfolk pines. Across the lake, on yet another tall esker, the white spire of the Methodist church stood stark against the backdrop of colorful trees. Lit by the sun, clean and white, it pointed its narrow finger to heaven, reminding me that death is a passing moment and but a doorway.

Surrounded by a profusion and jumble of autumn colors, I paused for a moment to drink in the sight. There is hope and new joy on the Distance Hill. I wondered if Bill had ever gotten the answer he sought before the Angel of Death took him away from us . . .

I smiled to myself and felt peace settle in upon me. Bill was not here on this side of the lake anymore. He was on the Distance Hill.

We passed softly through the old old section of the cemetery, past the ancient crypt where the mold and dampness hung perpetually; where the sounds of all life seemed to have been sucked from every molecule that hung miserably in the air around the metal doors. I felt the hair rise on my neck, and even the dogs were pulling to get away from this place. The legend was that a witch had been entombed here. She had threatened to curse the whole town if they did not bury her here.

We walked past the century old marker of Edward Schaude, husband of Myrtle Schaude, who poisoned him with strychnine and blamed his death on her lover. His body had been exhumed, and there stretched out on two sawhorses in the cemetery; a post mortem had been performed.

At the bottom of the hill, along the shore, the mist turned to a drizzle. The water lilies and purple flowering plants grew thick – so thick that a murderer thought he could leave a young woman to die here, some twenty years ago. On a cold and wet day such as this, she breathed her last breath, there amidst the water lilies.

Silently we walked the lower path, past the place where all the anglers used to cast their lines out past the water lilies. It was always the same group of anglers. They did not speak to each other but spread themselves out along the shore, each marking a spot, with small Styrofoam cups filled with dirt and worms. Nearly invisible strands of fishing line hung over rotting snags out past the water lilies. Even now, there remained a crook of a branch, pushed into the wet ground of the bank, waiting to cradle a fishing pole.

Ah yes. This spot, between the large willow and the purple spikes of marsh plants, the old couple had always fished. During the hot summer days, they brought out two battered plaid lawn chairs and an old dented cooler. She worn a tattered straw hat and he wore a dingy baseball cap, frayed along the brim and heavily stained with dark fingerprints. Often they sat side-by-side, not speaking a word, without fishing poles, just looking out across the yellow mass of water lilies that rounded the edge of the lake where the current ran stronger.

Peacefully they enjoyed the hum of the bees and the sudden plop when a fish sprang from the water to catch a mayfly. Silently, with their weathered hands entwined, they were comfortable with each other, and their love was indelibly written on each other's heart.

Sometimes they would sit and laugh with heads tipped back until a hat would drop to the ground. Oblivious to anyone who walked by, and to the other anglers along the shore, they enjoyed life calmly, peacefully... happily. Sometimes one would start a sentence while the other would finish it. It was obvious to me that as old and weathered as they were, inside, where the core of life resides, they were as happy as children were. They were soul mates. I often wondered how they came to be so much in love. . . all through these years together. I also wondered how they kept their love fresh and young.

It had been just about two weeks before the Cemetery Committee passed their decree that the couple suddenly stopped coming down to the shady spot beneath the big willow. I had thought at first that perhaps since the weather had begun to turn cooler in the mornings, that they were arriving later in the day when I had already walked through. Or, perhaps they had heard about the decree and had gone elsewhere to fish.

As I walked by, my heart leapt to my throat, for there stood the old man in his faded blue satin bowling jacket, alone. He stood with his back to me, to the big old willow tree and the thick swatch of water lilies in the lake, to face a fresh rectangle of ravished earth amidst the grave markers.

His baseball cap lay on the ground forgotten, and his shoulders, rounded in grief, clearly expressed his sorrow. I walked by swiftly, silently, hoping that I did not disturb him, and feeling the pain that radiated from him. He saw nothing about him, heard nothing, and fixed his eyes upon the patch of ground.

He let out a sob and lifted his eyes toward the top of the esker, past the white spire on the Distance Hill and cast a heartrending inquiry far out beyond the water lilies in the cold lake:

"I have asked You many times. Why. . .why? You have no answer for me?"

On the very last day before the degree took effect, I saw the old man once again standing with his back to the willow and the indifferent lake. The sod was now in place again. A small and delicate white stone marked the spot where the earth had been overturned.

The old man had lost weight; his clothes seemed to hang on him and his shoulders were stooped with an invisible load. He did not hear me for he was lost in conversation, whispering to the patch of earth in a halting cadence. His blue satin bowling jacket hung on his bony shoulders with the collar turned inward as though he had not noticed. She was not there to make it right for him anymore.

The wind had picked up and changed direction. The light drizzle was beginning to fall in larger drops and the lake had turned an icy charcoal color. It was time to go home. I shook my head and cleared my mind of the old couple that fished by the big willow.

Parked beneath the flowing branches of the willow, the car stood. It must have been there all night. The windows were open and the drizzling rain had turned the car seats dark. The dented blue cooler sat on the passenger's side and a soggy bag lay crumpled beside it with french fries carelessly spilled across the seat. The driver's door was slightly ajar.

I glanced across the path to where the small white gravestone stood and scanned the length of the cemetery as far as I could see. I was the only person in the world up and about at this time of the morning. He was not here. Perhaps the car had broken down last night and he had walked back into town.

"Let's go. . ." I called to the dogs. There was a new sadness to this place.

I pulled my hood down just a bit to keep the rain from falling directly onto my face, and turned away, back toward the path, shutting out the sight of everything about me. It was a wet and miserable day. Home. We would go home now.

The Border Collies had been straining to reach the shore where the water lilies grew the thickest. They watched only for a moment as the current carried a blue satin jacket out beyond the jumble of water lilies and out into the lake toward the Distance Hill.

Poor Stevie Ray Dog

He was certainly the most forlorn dog in the house. He was the most neglected. And, most obviously, to him, he was quite the most unnoticed dog in the bunch. So says Stevie Ray Dog.

"Might as well go out in the garden and eat worms."

(.... Except...the ground is frozen solid and it is now buried under a think layer of crusty hard snow).

" Ah well, can't even go out in the garden and eat worms."
        (We never have a garden either).

Poor Stevie Ray Dog. He lay with his head flat to the floor and his airplane wing ears spread out wide to emphasize the very flatness of

97

the sad state of things. Tilting his head ever so slightly, he gazed at her from just beyond the doorway of the office.

There was a heavy sigh. Mom has been just awful to Stevie Ray Dog. Perhaps she had not heard his heavy sigh. He picked himself up off the floor and trotted into the kitchen where she stood with her back to him. She appeared to be busy with something on the countertop. Stevie Ray Dog threw himself to the floor again with a clunk and let out another morose sigh.

First, she washed that wonderful smell off. You know the one. It is a good strong smell and sits in a crusty mess, entangled into the spiraling curls on his withers and rump. He had worked that smell in very carefully too, rolling about on his back and squirming with his hind legs pumping the air in a vigorous version of doggie aerobics.

And she removed it! Hauled him down to the basement and got him all wet and soapy. Several times too. Now he smelled...not like he wanted to smell. He did not have that strong "Manly Dog" smell anymore. It was replaced with that sissy dog smell.

She wears a different smell every once in awhile. Why couldn't he wear something different too?

And she took the butter away again. He had stretched himself up over the countertop as far as was dog-idly possible. He had nearly ejected his liver and spleen in that grand effort to stick his giraffe-like tongue across the length of the countertop and up over to the top of the toaster oven to reeeeach for the butter.

Just as he had gotten his little front teeth, and one big canine tooth hooked into that cold stick of butter, she had spotted him and had stormed in on him ... kind of like a one-woman swat team. She peeled his lips back, and told him point blank, in front of all the other doggies:

"DROP IT!"

How embarrassing. All he was able to taste of the butter was the tiny bit that had stuck to the inside of his canine tooth. Even then, as he was flipped his tongue in and out, in and out, she had glared at him. Put him in a down/stay and scowled at him when he started to get up. Humiliating!

After that, she took the knobby rubbery football away from him. He loves that football. She keeps it high up on a shelf and only brings it down when she is watching.

But she forgot about that football yesterday. And he hugged it, carried it around, pounced on it, tripped over it. Then she was mean and took it away from him. He had only gotten the chance to eat a third of it too. She said it was alarming to see multi-colored poop out in the backyard – and she was still trying to get over the sight of his last odd snack.

That must have been the day he ate the arm off that little plastic doll she had. He thought it looked sweet sitting up there on the shelf. Then he wondered if it tasted sweet too. The arm went down in one gulp – and then showed up the next day, sticking out of his poop with those little tiny fingers extended, as though to say:

"Somebody save us from Stevie Ray Dog!"

Personally, he thought it was rather creative – like an Artist's Statement. Sigh...

Poor Stevie Ray Dog.

What's that smell? Sniff sniff sniff...toast! She is making toast. Stevie loves toast. She is putting that butter on the toast.... and looks like she is removing a curly red hair from the butter. That must be Stevie's piece of toast - cuz that was his hair on it.

Oh, groan.... she is eating his toast! How come she can have the butter and he can't? Butter would make his coat shine so nice and pretty. He was just sure of it. Heck. Look at Cap! He gets into the butter more often – and his coat looks really great!

And then just before the last bite was about to disappear, she looked at him and handed him the toast.

"Poor Stevie Ray Dog," she said.

Stevie buried his face into her big sweatshirt and shut his eyes as he felt her hands run over his head and neck. They were small, gentle hands that had removed the burrs from his tail yesterday. The same hands that brushed him carefully and rubbed his ears. The same hands that gave him the peanut butter that stuck to the roof of his mouth. He put his front feet up onto her lap, rested his chin on her shoulder, and let her hair fall over his muzzle. She was whispering to him. He loved to hear her whisper to him.

"Poor Stevie Ray Dog."

Ring

"**Yes,** well Grace likes animals," my parents would say, as though this was some sort of abnormality I would outgrow. "Just wait 'til she's older. She'll forget about dogs and start thinking about boys. You know how that goes." The adults would share a nod of understanding. For some reason, when grownups get into that kind of conversation, they seem to think that kids not only don't understand the conversation going on, they can't hear, either.

Owning a dog was a very serious thing to me and I could never look at a dog without feeling there was more to a dog than what I had been told. I could see the thinking behind the eyes and had always wished that I could speak "Dog." Then I would know if the dog was happy with the way he was being treated. I was convinced that a dog would never give away my secrets or laugh at whatever silly thing I had to say. If I could speak Dog, we would really have something special and I could be my dog's savior when grownups just couldn't understand what my dog wanted and needed. Yup. Speaking Dog would be just about the best talent a person like me could want to have.

A Perfectly Good Dog

One hot Sunday afternoon in July, I sat on a step in the shade of the porch, feeling the coolness of the concrete against my legs. Beside me, panting from the heat, sat my uncle's Border Collie, Ring. Somewhat bored, I cast about for something to idle away the time. My mind wandered back to the sermon my grandfather had given at church that morning.

Grandpa was a stern man who never smiled, and perhaps this had been one of the reasons why he frightened me. He also had gnarled hands with fingers that curled like claws. Arthritis, they said. For some reason I could never understand, he liked to reach out and poke me in the tummy with one of those gnarled fingers. The skin on his hands were rough and patchy from years of hard toil, and he had a pigment problem which resulted in some of his fingers looking pink while the rest of his hands were suntanned and spotted. The combination of the odd coloration, the claw-like fingers with their knobby knuckles reminded me of the clawed feet on our cast iron bathtub.

Grandpa was formidable and with his puritan sternness, he had pushed the idea into his sons that God was stern rather than loving. The entire family regarded him as a pillar whose favorite theme in life was "Thou shalt not steal." To him, borrowing, touching, promising to return a borrowed object and being slow about it, all amounted to some degree of stealing. To handle or play with someone else's possession was also stealing, and to think about wanting that possession was the next step that lead to stealing. Yes, he was imposing. He lived right next door with my uncle and aunt, and I did my best to stay out of his way.

Grandpa spent most of his time out in the garden with a hoe. On many occasions I had seen him on his knees in the sun-warmed dirt, not pulling up weeds or picking vegetables – but praying. He would shake his head and raise his gnarled hands to the sky. I was certain that he had a direct connection to God because he had said right there in church "I love the Lord and the Lord loves me." So God loves stern old grandpas who poke little kids and who never smiles?

The sermon had covered two topics. The first one I didn't understand very well, but the second one had been about going to heaven and I knew I wanted Ring with me. I repeated the sermon to him, just to make sure he knew the rules to get to heaven.

"Ring, now that you're a grown up dog and getting old, I think it's time you knew about heaven. Are you listening, Ring? Don't be looking off at the crows in the cornfield. This is very important. So pay attention."

Ring lowered his body to the cool concrete and half closed his eyes while the end of his tongue dripped a small puddle between his front paws.

"On Sundays, Ring, we go to church and listen to a sermon. It's a different sermon every Sunday, and a lot of times, I just don't get it. But today, I think I understood nearly all of it. Well...all except the first part about Stewart's ship. I don't know who Stewart is – but maybe his ship is how you get to heaven. That must be it, because the minister said it was what the church depended on. I'll skip that part."

"Anyway, heaven is the best place you'd ever want to be, Ring. It's better than here, and it's better than anything you can think of and when you get really old and die, heaven is the place you want to go. But. Just because you die, it doesn't mean you automatically go there. You have to be a good dog all your life. Not just good when people are watching you or when it's easy to be good – but all the time, inside yourself and outside too. That means no growling, no stealing the cat's food and no peeing on Uncle's boots when he's not wearing them. If you can't be a really good dog all the time, then Jesus will forgive you. You just have to pray and ask Him."

I bent over and looked into Ring's face. I assumed he had closed his eyes in prayer and was concentrating so hard, he looked like he was asleep. I gave him a nudge.

"So d'you want to go to heaven with me, Ring?" I asked when I had concluded. I held out my hand and Ring slapped his paw into my open palm. "OK then. It's a deal. Have you sinned, Ring? Because if you have, then we have to take care of that first. You're a really good dog. I think Jesus thinks so too."

The screen door creaked open and Dad stepped out onto the shady stoop beside me, pretending that he did not notice me sitting there near his feet. He shaded his eyes and looked out into the pasture. I followed his gaze and watched the heat waves create wavy shapes out of the cattle and the distance apple orchard. A rush of dust scuttled across the property and disappeared into the line of scrub trees.

"What are you doing, Gracie?" he asked with just a twitch of a smile.

"Just talking to Ring, Daddy."

"Sunday sermon?"

"Yep. Ring is a good dog and it'd be a real shame if he didn't get to heaven, wouldn't it. So I was telling him how."

"I see… you know, some folks say only people go to heaven. Not dogs."

"Why?!"

"Because a dog doesn't have a soul."

"How do you know? Does the Bible say so, Daddy?"

"Well no… but everybody just knows."

"But if the Bible doesn't say so, and you can't see a soul, then how do you know that for sure, Daddy? I don't want to go to heaven if

104

dogs can't go there! What fun would that be? And besides, why would God make such a nice dog like Ring if He didn't think about taking him to heaven?"

"Personally, Gracie, I think that dogs go to their own heaven. A very special place without people. Where they have all their dog friends with them, and no people telling them what they can or cannot do."

"Think so? Then I want to go there, too."

Dad rattled his head, realizing that this was not a conversation he would be able to resolve easily.

"I'm surprised you remembered all of the sermon today, Gracie."

"Daddy, did you remember all of the sermon too?"

"Erm.... Well, most of it."

"Daddy, I think you would remember more of the sermon if you didn't spend so much of your time praying with your eyes closed while the minister is preaching."

He cleared his throat and shifted his weight.

"I'll try to remember that next Sunday... Did your mom see me ... praying?" He glanced nervously back toward the kitchen.

"Yes. She had her eyebrows all pushed down and she looked kind of crabby."

The heat of July was upon us and the grownups disappeared inside to the cool comforts of air conditioning. Life outdoors now belonged to me ... and Ring.

The following day my eyes landed on Ring. He often wandered over to our house to flop down under the cool shade of the big elm tree.

105

From this vantage point, he could keep an eye on what happened at both houses. Ring spent his days outside and his evenings sleeping in the kitchen. He had food and water and that was about it. No one paid any attention to him, and as much as Ring intrigued me, I was often chastised for interacting with him.

"He's not your dog! Leave him alone!"

"But Daddy, he likes me and he wants to be with me."

"He's not your dog. Do as I say, Gracie. Don't bother him. You grandpa wouldn't want you bothering Ring either."

One afternoon Ring stood eyeing me with his tongue hanging out long like a strip of raw liver. "I knew it!" I whispered to Ring as I picked up his water can. "Its empty. You should be my dog, Ring. I can take better care of you than uncle and auntie can. I just know it." I turned the spigot on and let the water overflow into the coffee can. Ring lapped at the running water until he was satisfied, then loped behind me to the shade of our elm tree.

My eyes ran over the length of his body. Large clumps of loose fur hung on him. He was really shedding. I picked a loose tuft of fur off his hip and watched his skin quivered as the fur came free. Hm... looks like Ring would be a lot cooler if he did not have all that loose fur on him. I went into the house and found an old comb.

For the rest of the afternoon I combed through Ring's coat, carefully removing mats, burs and large puffs of fur. Ring stood patiently with his eyes half closed while his thick coat gradually thinned out and floated away on the light summer breeze. The transformation was remarkable. He looked as though he had lost ten pounds. Now shining and tangle-free, Ring grinned at me and happily trotted off in the direction of home, disappearing around the north end of the house.

I felt that I had done a good and kind thing. Tired, my arms coated in a fine layer of oily dust, I picked up the old comb. The breeze had blown a tuft of Ring's fur onto my foot. I had been so intent on relieving Ring of his excess coat, that I had not noticed how much of it now lay about me under the tree.

A sudden breeze blew a flurry of Ring's fur across our side lawn, across the gravel driveway, across my uncle's lawn and into the pasture behind our two homes. Everywhere I looked, twigs and shrubs were festooned with black and white tufts of fur.

"Uh oh...I think I'm going to be in trouble."

I quietly slipped into the house, washed up very thoroughly and cleaned the comb to the best of my ability. I threw myself on my bed. Perhaps the breeze would carry all the fur farther out into the pasture, where nobody would notice it, before Daddy came home from work - or, before uncle came home from work. I picked up a book and flipped through the pages as though I could read - but my ears were tuned to the crunching sounds of a car coming up the driveway.

Creeping over to the window, I slowly raised my head high enough to peek out. Hidden from sight behind the lace curtains, I watched uncle's car roll to a stop. The door opened and he emerged. In his hand, he held his empty lunch box and a rumpled shirt. He stretched his arms out behind him and tipped his face toward the clear blue sky while he yawned broadly. A tuft of fur floated past his feet. Not noticing it, he turned and entered his house. I let out a sigh of relief.

"Well, I guess there's nothing to worry about." I smiled to myself and was just turning away from the window when uncle came back out of the house again. He walked halfway across the lawn and put his fists on his hips while he slowly turned to look at the fur clinging to every stick and branch, to the peony bushes, and tall grass that designated the start of the pasture. Reaching down, he picked up a long strand of fur and studied it for a moment. He picked up another. And another. When he had gathered a large handful, he stood up, considered the whole expanse of fur everywhere and let it all fall from his hand.

His head turned toward my bedroom window and I ducked out of sight. I crept along under the window and poked an eye out from the opposite side. Uncle was still standing there in the lawn, scratching his scalp. Finally, he turned to re-enter his house.

Logic suggested to me that this probably was not the end of things.

An hour later, the familiar hum from our old Ford drifted through the screened window of my bedroom. Every car I could ever remember being parked in our garage had been a Ford. And every car that been in uncle's garage had been a Chevy. There had been many conversations between my father and my uncle about which car manufacturer produced the better car. Usually, the conversations, in the form of debates, took place in the garage with one of them underneath a car and a pile of tools were scattered about within arm's reach.

"I see you've got car problems again. What's wrong with it this time? Ya know if you'd a bought a Chevy, you'd save yourself a big chunk of time and money. Look all what you've spent repairing that Ford," my uncle would say quite righteously as he squatted near the bumper to talk to Daddy's legs which were still visible. Other times, the conversation was reversed.

"Who was that that brought you home today? And where's your Chevy? Still having problems with that same thing? You never have that kind of problem with a Ford. Never."

They were brothers, like minded, and when they got in a humorous mood, I had difficulty following the humor for it seemed to be deeply rooted into their shared past. It was at these times that a slight Kentucky accent would develop out of nowhere. They held the same principles – the ones that grandpa had taught them.

I hopped off the bed and peeked out the window once again. The Ford slowed to a crawl halfway down the driveway, and I could see my father's head swivel from side to side.

The Ford came up to a stop at the garage and uncle stepped out of his house. The two men stood there in the driveway talking in low tones. Uncle picked a tuft of fur and handed it to Daddy.

Ten minutes later Daddy strolled into the bedroom and sat down on the edge of my bed. I lay on the floor, very busy, with two sets of doll outfits. He did not look like he was mad at me - but I could detect the Parental Conversational Sly Approach beginning.

"And what did you today, Gracie?" he asked.

"Not much. Pretty much the usual stuff." I replied in the Child's Conversational Defense Mode. "What did you do today, Daddy?"

"I did pretty much the usual stuff today too, honey." He sighed and I could see his tired eyes drift off toward the memory of his workday.

"Daddy, how do they decide how to pay you?" (Diversion tactic).

"Well… this week I am getting paid by piece rate."

"Peace Rate? You don't get paid if you get mad at somebody at work?"

"Not P-E-A-C-E rate. P-I-E-C-E rate. I get paid for each piece that I make." The twinkle came back into his eyes.

"Oh. Did you make a lot of pieces today?"

"It sure felt like it…"

"Daddy, when you're making all those pieces, and after you've got a bunch of them piled up, did you ever think to yourself: 'well, that just bought a head of cabbage.'"

Wearily he shook his head.

"No, I've never thought about it like that. And thank God I haven't because that is a very depressing thought." Too smart to be fooled by my attempt at misdirection, he went on.

"What else did you do today Gracie? Were you the one who brushed Ring today?"

"Why Daddy, how did you know it was me?"

"Who else could it possibly be? You love the animals more than anybody I know, and it just sounds like something you would do. Did you brush Ring today?" (Direct Approach accompanied by Compliment).

"Yes I did - and did you see how great he looks now? I'll bet they never brushed him all year. There were big tangles in his fur, Daddy, and some of them were pulling his skin. It must have hurt. They don't take very good care of Ring, Daddy. Did you know that I put water in his coffee can every day? Because he never has water and it's so hot. Don't you think that's just cruel and very selfish, Daddy? They're supposed to take care of him but they don't a very good job of it. And I get yelled at every time I take care of him. Auntie doesn't even let him inside the screen porch. And his water bowl is inside the screen porch and he can't even get to it to drink it. I put the big coffee can out by the spigot so Ring can have water whenever he needs it. Did you see how pretty Ring looks today, Daddy? He was really really happy to get all that hot hair off."

My father sat there quietly on the edge of the bed with his hands folded in his lap. He didn't say a word. Finally, he let out a sigh and looked out the window at the lawn and the fur.

"Gracie, I understand why you brushed Ring – and I was unaware of your other reasons for taking care of Ring. As I've said before, he is not your dog. Here's what I'm going to do. I'll go over and have a talk with your uncle. If your uncle promises to make some good changes for Ring, can you promise to leave Ring alone?"

It was a sad thought to leave Ring alone. I doubted that Ring wanted to be left alone. It was just in him to be with people. I was being asked to make a promise to leave him...alone. Grownups are really big on making promises to little kids until they thought they were too busy, or the promise was annoyingly difficult to keep, or they simply forget. Could I really turn my head away and watch Ring being left alone?

"I'm not sure I can promise that, Daddy."

"Why not?"

"Because I don't think Uncle could keep his end of the promise. I'm afraid he'll forget and then nobody will look out for Ring. But if he can keep his promise, then I can keep mine. Don't you think that's fair, Daddy?"

Once again, he was staring at me as if he could not believe I was his offspring. Without another word, he got up and walked out of the

111

room. I heard the back door open and close, his footsteps pass my window, and the tired man walked over to uncle's house.

I threw myself back on the bed again and thought about this. Perhaps it would be a good idea to make some sort of gesture on my part, indicating that I would attempt to keep my end of that promise. Really, the whole point of this was the fur all over the place. I doubted that giving Ring water was an issue with Uncle. It had to be the fur. He wanted it on the dog and not on the lawn. I decided that I would pick up all the floating fur after supper that evening.

Later, when the damp coolness of the evening began to set in, I armed myself with a brown paper bag, intent on collecting the dog hair. By now, the fur had spread everywhere. As I picked up the fur around the elm tree, I had the sensation of being watched. Looking over at my uncle's house, I saw the kitchen curtain suddenly fall back into position.

So...he was watching me. I could just picture him sitting there in the cool semi-light of his kitchen, thinking that he was hidden, watching me. I wondered what he thought of my effort, and how long he would sit there. I picked up fur until the bag was about half full - but I had barely cleared the ground under the elm tree. I sighed. There was still nearly half an acre of land dotted with fur.

Wisps of fur that waved like little flags off the tops of dried out twigs, more wisps had floated up into the willow tree, and clung to the electric fence at the edge of the pasture. I should have brushed Ring and put the fur into a bag right away instead of letting it fly away on the hot summer wind.

If the wind shifted direction to the west, by tomorrow evening our grouchy neighbor would be calling about the fur all over the vegetables in his garden.

And what of Ring? Would these grownups come to a decision that since I could not leave Ring along, Ring would have to go? Had I jeopardized his life because I tried to do a good thing for a nice dog? Would they regard all the fur as evidence that I had intention in my heart of stealing Ring? If so, the best thing to do to save my soul, would be to remove the temptation. Would they take him to the shelter? Would they take him away and never bring him back again? What had I done!

A sense of urgency came over me, and then despair. It was too dark to collect all that fur - and by tomorrow morning, it would spread even further across the landscape. It was time to call for some real help.

"Jesus…" I lifted my eyes up and looked through the branches of the elm tree. The first hints of stars were beginning to appear in the early evening sky. Somewhere up there, He was watching me and understood. "Did I make a mistake? Was it a bad one? I only wanted to do a good thing and now I'm scared. I don't know what to do, Jesus. I know You're really busy, and this may not seem like a big deal - but to me it is. Please…can You fix this?"

The vastness of the universe spread out above me, making me feel smaller and more helpless than ever. Did He hear me? I could not tell, and there was nothing else I could do; there was nothing else I could think of that could possibly make a difference. I picked myself up, brushed off my knees, and went back inside the house feeling as though I had swallowed a large rock.

I slept badly, tossing and turning until the sheets were tangled like a thick rope. When the first streaks of gold and rose-colored light broke upon the bedroom walls, I was finally sleeping very soundly. My father and uncle both left for work, but I slept on, not hearing their cars crunch down the gravel driveway. Perhaps my mother knew I was upset and let me sleep, for when I finally crawled out of bed, I discovered that I had missed breakfast.

Afraid to go outside and look at what the wind had done with the fur, I spent the entire day moping about in my bedroom, pretending to have fun with a load of crayons lined up like odd little soldiers on the pale carpet. My coloring book lacked the enthusiasm I normally poured into each drawing. Today, my heart just was not in it. I had decided that I would talk to my uncle and explain to him that I was only trying to help, and that I had made a mistake. Surely, he would understand.

All too soon, I heard his car door slam, and I scrambled to catch him before he went into his house. To my surprise, he walked across our lawn, headed for our back door. I realized that I had not prepared my opening statement. I shoved my hands into the pockets of my shorts and stood there in center of the dusty little path worn into the ground between the two houses.

He was going to lecture me. OK...I had it coming. He wouldn't spank me since I was not his little kid. I stood as tall as I could and waited for him.

Very briefly, his eyes flickered to mine. He cleared his throat, looked away, and cleared his throat again.

"Gracie, I had a long talk with your Dad yesterday, and he explained how you see things... from your point of view. I didn't realize that you were only trying to help. I promise you, Gracie, I will do my very best to take better care of Ring. I'll put a dog door into the porch so he can get nice cool water whenever he wants it, and he'll be able to get out of the hot sun. This weekend we'll give him a bath, and today I stopped at the store and bought a brush. I watched you picking up the fur in the yard last night. That was a very nice thing to do. It must have taken you hours! Thank you, Gracie."

"You're welcome," I said, stunned.

He turned on his heel and, flinging his work shirt over his shoulder, went back to his own house. It was the first time I could ever remember a grownup making a serious promise to me.

I turned and faced the elm tree. I slowly turned a complete circle. There was not a bit of dog fur to be seen anywhere. It had vanished!

"Jesus!" I gasped in surprise as I tipped my face up to the azure blue sky. "You heard me!"

I couldn't refrain from skipping back down the dusty little path toward my house. Just as I reached for the doorknob, a new thought came to me: "I should say thank you properly."

I needed to get as close to heaven as I could, to say a proper thank you, and for that, I needed to climb my special tree. I sprinted off across the field, ducked under the electric fence and ran down the east fence line. Small scrub crab apple trees, wild rose bushes and tall elephant grass delineated the property line more clearly than the rusty barbed wire fence. Ring was safe, he would get better care than he had been getting, and I was not in trouble after all.

The Prayer Tree had a smooth, silky, greenish gray bark, with pleasantly supple limbs. It was my favorite tree because it swayed so beautifully in the wind.

When the summer storms turned the sky a dark charcoal color, and the winds would howl across the fields of clover and wheat, I would race back to my tree and climb as high as I could. I would wrap my legs firmly around a limb and throw my arms wide to the sky where the wind caused the branches to swing wildly back and forth. The joy of the wind rushing past my ears, the rustling leaves and the illusion of being able to fly was so wonderful, I would sing at the top of my lungs with my eyes closed. I sang for joy, for the inner peace, for the thrill of being nearly able to fly.

Sometimes I would reach up, hold my arms out to God, wishing He could pick me up, and hold me just for a little while. As the first fat drops of rain began to splatter down through the branches, before the limbs became too slippery to hold, I would clamber down the tree as quickly as I could and race back home.

I dashed past the scrub trees, scooted through the hole in the line of brush, and came to an abrupt stop. My mouth fell open as I looked at the line of thickly tangled vegetation hiding the barbed wire fence. Bird nests! Woven into the greens and dusty grays of the thorny crab apple trees, they were nearly invisible. Each nest was neatly wrapped in the soft black, cream and browns of Ring's fur.

"So that's how You did it ...."

The rest of the summer passed at a snail's pass. By the beginning of August, my sister Ella and I ran out of things to do and started spending a lot of time inside. Mother complained about the backdoor constantly slamming, the heat of outside invading the coolness of the inside, the floors getting dirtier, and told us we had to make a choice: Inside or outside. Not both. We chose inside. However, the constant pattering of our feet up and down the hallway got on her nerves and she eventually shooed us outside.

"Don't come in until supper time!"

Searching for something to do, we remembered the old cast iron bathtub. Dad and Uncle had heaved the lovely cast iron tub out of the house and replaced it with a pale blue fiberglass one. It was modern and sleek, and void of the charm that radiated from the cast iron tub. Styles had changed and the era of Formica was upon us. The cast iron tub now sat amidst the tall grass and scrub crab apple bushes, just behind the chicken coop.

My older sister, Ella, confided in me that she was very glad the old tub was out of the house. The feet had always frightened her. At the sloping end of the tub, the feet looked like giant scaly reptile claws clutching a ball. I tried to picture the large talons slowly flexing over the ball. Perhaps it was not intended to be the feet of a bird but rather, a dragon. It was these very dragon thoughts that frightened her.

"Ella, are you still afraid of the tub?"

"Yes! It's even scarier now that it's out here in the tall grass. Every time the wind blows through the grass and makes that hissing sound, I get goose bumps. It's the feet, you know. They're really scary."

I studied the feet once more and tried picturing the tub suddenly walking. The legs were much too short - and there was no head. How in the world could she find this scary? I thought it was marvelous. Scared or not, Ella was willing to play in the tub with me. She was an odd combination of courage and fear.

I sat down on the edge of the tub and drummed my fingers, listening to the hollow echo. Sweat trickled down between my shoulder blades and I thought about running back to the house for something cool to drink. It was a very hot day.

"How about the tub being an igloo?" I asked, thinking about the white coldness of snow

"An igloo? How's that gonna work?" Ella asked.

"We tip it over."

"...I don't know. It's pretty heavy. What if we can't turn over again?"

"Well...let's try a practice. We'll be on the outside and if we can put it upright from the outside, then we know we can do it over from the inside."

"Ok."

Careful not to roll the tub over onto our feet, we pushed mightily on one side and the tub rolled over. Next we stood side by side and heaved the tub back upright again. Panting hard, we sat on the edge of the tub to catch our breath before we turned it over on ourselves.

"Are you ready?"

"Yup."

With a great deal of effort, we turned the tub over on ourselves and giggled, as we had the best hiding place ever. Hidden at the edge of the property line and nearly buried in the tall grass, nobody would think to look for us here!

Ella, being two years older and a head taller, sat with her head crooked to the side at an uncomfortable angle. I sat with my legs crossed, ducking just a bit. We chatted and gleefully sang while our voices bounced about the hard surface.

The interior was dimly lit by the cracks of light seeping in along the dry ground and through the holes where the fixtures would have been. Being at the fixture end, I put my eye to the hole and peered out. The grass blocked my view and all I could hear was the hissing sound that frightened Ella.

We had thought that the shadowy interior would be cooler but the rough black bottom of the tub was now facing the sun. The space under the tub was growing hotter and hotter. It wasn't so much fun. It was time to leave.

"I don't like this anymore. Let's get out of here," Ella said.

The tub had somehow become very heavy. I had thought that I would just put my back to the top of the tub and use my back to help turn the tub over – but I was too small. I got onto my hands and knees and discovered that I was still a couple inches short from touching my back to the tub. I tried getting to my feet but there was not enough room to squat. I squeezed my fingers under the rim where the cracks of light illuminated our plight, and tried to help lift the tub with my fingers. It was hopeless and Ella was not strong enough to flip the tub over alone. We tried and tried to free ourselves until we were both too exhausted to do anything but huddle on our knees, panting.

We were trapped. Sweat dampened out cotton shirts and plastered our hair to our faces. It was hard to breath. The space began to close in and I started to cry. It was so hot. Black flowers began to blossom in front of my eyes. My big sister, always strong, always there for me, began to cry too. Panic flooded my chest, choking out reason, oxygen and hope. Even though I was at the end of the tub with the fixture holes, I was sure we would run out of air and die.

We screamed for help but our voices only bounced about inside the hot iron tub. Mom and Dad were inside the house, half an acre away. They would never hear us.

I put my mouth up to the fixture hole and screamed for help while Ella covered her ears. We waited tearfully and no one came to help us. I tried again. And I tried again. Ella sobbed hysterically.

"We're going to die in here and nobody will ever know where to find our bodies!"

I screamed for help through the small hole one more time as the vision of someone finding us days or weeks later flashed through my vivid imagination.

In sheer desperation, I stuck my arm through the hole and waved it frantically, hoping somebody had heard my screams and was looking for us. Coolness and the freedom were within reach. I wished with all my heart that I could push the rest of me out of the small hole. I would run home and get Dad, and he would turn the tub over to free Ella. Stretching my arm up as high as I could, all I felt was the radiated heat from the cast iron tub. Would anyone see my arm in the waving prairie grass? Would anyone even think to look this direction?

Ella began reciting Psalms 23 while she rocked back and forth. I curled myself up into the smallest ball that I could, hoping a little extra space would help her feel better about our forthcoming death. Resting my forehead against the hot surface, I closed my eyes and tried to shut out Ella's droning. It felt like a very long time - but it might have only been minutes. Time has a funny way of changing speed at the most uncomfortable times.

"Shh!" I hissed over Ella's sobs. "I think I hear something!"

I put my ear to the hole and heard a faint rustling of the grass. Once again, I stuck my arm out and felt ....fur! Startled, I pulled my arm back in quickly. To my great surprise, following my hand back inside the tub, came Ring's black and white muzzle. The black nose wiggled and sniffed. He let out a deafening bark of excitement to have found us.

"Ring! Go get help! Go get help!" I pushed his nose back out the hole. He stood there for a moment looking confused and then, with reluctance, Ring disappeared. Ella burst into tears again.

"What a stupid dog. He doesn't know what to do. He's not Lassie, you know! He's just a dumb dog! We're going to die in here." She buried her face in her hands, sobbing again.

I thought she was probably right about Ring. He definitely was not Lassie. Ring had never been expected to do anything in his entire life. He had never been trained to do anything except stay in the yard. He was ... just a dog.

I put my ear to the hole and heard Ring barking and barking off in the distance. Where had he gone? Had he forgotten us? Did he understand that we were in a horrible situation and we needed help? Maybe I should had held his collar and tried to get him to bark right there outside the tub. Then someone would have noticed him and come. Why oh why hadn't I thought of that! Doubts began flooding my head. Now it was too late and Ring was beyond my reach.

The barking stopped and my heart sank. We were alone and without help again. I curled up into a ball again and took slow breaths of the hot air. Ella would not answer me anymore. She was in her own world and had left me. I closed my eyes, tuned out the sound of Ella's sobs, and waited for the end. Gradually she grew very quiet. I was afraid to look at her, thinking she might have died from the heat. We lay silently in our iron tomb with the heat smothering us.

Suddenly the tub flipped itself over! Glaring sunlight exploded around us and the excessive heat wafted away. Startled, we both sat there blinking and shielding our eyes. The first thing I saw was my father's boots - and the second thing I saw was Ring smiling at me with his tail waving proudly.

Ring had run to our house. He had bounced off the door, barking and barking until my father came out to see what the matter was. Once he had stepped out the door, Ring had urged him to follow him. He circled and herded him over to the bathtub, and once the overturned tub came into sight, my father knew who he would find beneath the tub – and hoped that he was not too late.

For the rest of Ring's life, I was allowed the privilege of his companionship without asking permission to be with him or to care for him. Wisps of fur across the lawn and driveway were never frowned on again. In fact, the fur brought smiles to the grownups' faces and solemn conversations about how good it was to have a dog like Ring to watch over the children. I spent the rest of the summer joyously running through the fields of clover with Ring bounding along beside me. He waited patiently at the base of my Prayer Tree looking up at me while I climbed to the very top. I threw my hands high to the sky.

"Jesus! You heard me. I needed Your help …and so did Ring." I somberly shook my head; amazed at the way the He had worked it all out.

Eddy's Dog

Thea's long day finally ended and now it was time to go home. It seemed it did not matter how many hours she put in at work. There was still too much for her to get done in a day. But that was how life was, and now it was time to go home. A rasping cough drained a little more strength from her as she lowered her tall thin frame into the old car. She cautiously sucked in a shallow lungful of air. The cough returned with a vengeance. Thea leaned her head against the steering wheel and blinked away the twinges of pain that still lingered in her chest.

"Guess I better go see the doc some time soon . . ." She muttered to herself as the car rumbled to life. "Right now, I just wanna go home and put my feet up." The car slowly left the parking lot, and headed for the end of town.

"Ah nuts!" Thea shook her head. "I have to get some groceries. And dog food." She turned the car back into town. A light mist had begun to fall. Pools of light created patches of shiny black obsidian at the foot of each streetlight. Squinting through the partially fogged windshield, she gradually slowed down as a dark figure staggered along the side of road. It was Eddy. Why was he walking home? Where was his jacket? And where was his car?

Eddy carried a battered lunch box with nearly indiscernible Star Wars figures on it. The right pocket of his stained khaki pants was turned inside out and waving like a little flag. He dropped his thermos and stopped to stare at it for a few seconds, as though this would put the object back into his hands. Slowly and deliberately, he spread his feet wide for stability and leaned forward to reach for it, like a giraffe getting a drink of water. With his fingertips just a few inches from the thermos, his knees suddenly buckled and Eddy fell to the pavement, striking his forehead on the thermos.

Thea shook her head and brought her car to a stop next to the sidewalk. She rolled the window down and calmly called out.

"Eddy, its me. Thea. Want a ride home?"

Eddy rolled onto his back and pulled his head up to look at Thea. He straightened his shirt from his horizontal position and gave Thea a little wave.

"Eddy, where's you car?" Thea asked as she helped Eddy off the pavement and into her car. He gave her a sheepish grin and mumbled through fumes of alcohol that he has lost his license. He was walking for a while. Thea shook her head and thought to scold him - but she knew it would do no good tonight.

"Thea?" the tiny voice came over the phone. "Its me, Beth. Thea, I know you aren't feeling good right now - but you gotta do something about Eddy's dog. Thea, he's killing her." Beth broke down in tears.

"What do you mean he's killing her, Beth? Not Eddy. Sure he's a drunk - but he doesn't have a mean bone in his body. I didn't even know Eddy had a dog. Are you sure?"

"Yes, Thea. He's got a black and white dog. I don't know what you call 'em. You know, the kind you see on the farms all the time. Medium size with a white ring around her neck. I know you've got a house full of dogs right now. But could you just take one more? Thea, please. Go talk to Eddy and get that dog from him. He's killing her. She's so skinny. I don't think he feeds her enough."

"All right. I'll give him a call. You must be talking about a Border Collie. Those dogs usually are thin, Beth."

"No Thea. This one is really skinny. I'm scared for her. Please Thea, get that dog from Eddy. He likes you and he trusts you. Just get that dog from him?"

"I have a doctor's appointment in about a half hour. I'll stop by Eddy's place right after that."

Thea had no time for a visit to the doctor. The county she lived in had no animal shelter and she was trying to get one going. It was just a small group of people who met every couple of weeks - for now. However, they were making progress. Soon, she hoped. Soon. In the meantime, she had eight dogs and she adopted them out as she could. She thought on these things as she waited for the doctor to come back with the chest x-rays. Her long slender legs dangled from the end of the examining table while she drummed impatient rhythms with her fingertips. Why was it, she asked herself, doctors always spoke to you as though you were deaf?

"Thea," the doctor swung the door open and stuffed an x-ray into the light box that hung on the wall. "You have to slow down and rest. Right now, you have pneumonia. See this? " He stuck a finger into the x-ray.

"Doc, I don't have time right now - "

"No Thea. You HAVE to slow down. You're going to end up in the hospital."

"Hospital! . . . Naw! Anyway, I can't stay in a hospital. I've got eight dogs to take care of and a farm to run."

"Thea," the doctor's eyebrows ran together, "you won't have a choice. You WILL end up in the hospital by no choice of your own. And then who will take care of things? You have to slow down and take better care of yourself."

"Okay. I can probably cut my work hours down a bit . . . and I'll go to bed earlier . . . and what else?"

Eddy was not home. Thea walked around the apartment, peering into the windows that she could reach. The apartment was very dark inside. In fact, it gave her the impression that nobody lived there. She didn't see a dog. Maybe it was in the garage. No garage door windows. The garage door was locked. Thea rapped on the garage door thinking if the dog was in there, it might start barking. Nothing. Not a sound. She'd have to call Eddy later tonight. No, he'll be too drunk by then. She'd catch him at work tomorrow and talk to him then.

Beth had a tendency to exaggerate. Maybe Eddy's dog was just one of those thin Border Collies. Thea closed her eyes and pictured Beth's two fat Westies. They were happy bouncy dogs, pampered, taken everywhere, and too fat. Most dogs would look somewhat thin next to those Westies. Overly fat wasn't good for a dog either.

126

Thea tried for the next week to talk Eddy into giving her the dog. Eddy said he loved that dog. She was a good dog. Never got into nothing, never barked. She was a good dog. He hung his head sadly at the idea of giving his good dog away. She was his friend, ya know. And besides, right now, he really needed his friend. Cuz he lost his drivers license and just yesterday, he lost his apartment too.

"Well Eddy, how about I just keep her with me for awhile. Just 'til you get back on your feet again. How about it, Eddy?" She had asked. But Eddy had shook his head and had reluctantly walked away. There wasn't much she could do about it. Besides, he promised her he would take care of the dog. And if he couldn't, he knew she was there.

Now she was worried. The more she thought about it, the more she was worried. Through the rest of the day, thoughts about Eddy's dog drifted through her mind and destroyed her concentration. Eddy was not going to give her the dog. He was too ashamed. She would have to come up with another way.

That evening as she made a cup of hot tea, Thea stewed on the idea of how to get the dog from Eddy. She paced back and forth through the kitchen with a collection of dogs following her. Her Aussie circled and followed her, eyes dancing with delight. Thea kicked a tennis ball through the living room doorway and watched as the Aussie returned with the ball and dropped it at her feet. She sent the ball out again.

"That's it! Send the ball out. Yes! I'll send a ball out. George. I'll send George out to talk to Eddy!" Thea spoke excitedly to the dogs.

127

She picked up the phone and called George, explaining the situation. An hour later George called back.

"Okay Thea," George said flatly. "I went out to Eddy's place and saw his dog and I had a long talk with Eddy. If you want that skinny dog, she's yours. But you had better go get her tonight before Eddy changes his mind again. He's expecting you to come."

Thea thanked George and rushed out the door while she put on her coat. The hacking cough returned, reminding her that she had promised the doctor that she would slow down. She dropped behind the steering wheel and thought for a few seconds. She needed a leash probably. Was there one in the car? The dome light flickered briefly and went out. She rapped on it, nudging it back into life.

"I gotta get that fixed some time soon."

Eddy was standing outside when she drove up. He hung his head low, not able to look Thea in the eye. He turned and invited her into his mother's house. Inside were boxes and boxes of Eddy's belongings, all in various stages of being sorted through and emptied. He offered her a beer. She declined saying she was driving. Maybe on another visit, though. Where was the dog?

Eddy led her out to the dank garage and gave a whistle. From back in a dark corner Thea could hear the click of toenails. And then a delicate shape slowly walked out from under a tarp to sit in front of Eddy. Not a sound from the dog except for a light swish swish of the tail. The smell of a dirty dog rose to her nose. Eddy reached behind him and took a hunk of cotton clothesline from the wall. He looped it

128

around the dog's neck and handed the free end to Thea. Without a word, he turned and slowly walked back into the house.

Thea strained to see through the gloom for a better look at the dog. Too dark in here. Clucking, she coaxed the dog from the garage and opened the car door.

"Come sweet baby! Up!" She patted the seat and the quiet dog thought for a moment before hopping in. Thea rapped on the dome light again- but this time it could not be coaxed to life.

"Guess I'm gonna have to get that fixed now, right sweet baby?" she cooed to the lump of dog that had sunk out of sight on the dark floor. "Don't worry, girl. I've got you now. You'll be okay with me."

Thea let out a sigh of relief. Finally. She had the dog. Eddy had told her the dog's name was Zoey. All during the drive home, she considered which order to do things in. Zoey would have to see the vet about her vaccinations. Zoey needed a bath! She forgot to ask Eddy what brand of dog food he was feeding her. And all the while, Zoey laid very still and quiet on the floor. Was she frightened? Was she confused? Was she a good dog like Eddy said?

Thea pulled into her driveway and smiled as she heard the excited sounds of greeting coming from her own dogs. In the window, perched on the couch like a cat, sat her little Schnauzer. Hopping up and down, then out of sight, was her own Border Collie. She would have to put them in the bedroom until she had gotten Zoey comfortable inside.

The car rolled to a stop and still Zoey made no sound or movement. Slowly, her head came up as she sensed they had arrived somewhere. Thea opened the passenger side door cautiously and picked up the end of the cotton line.

"Come Zoey. Come sweet girl!"

Delicately and carefully, the shadowy shape slid out of the car. With head hanging low, Zoey followed Thea into the bright lights of the warm kitchen.

"Here we go Zoey dear! Now you'll have a ---!"

Thea let out a gasp of horror. She stood motionless for what seemed an eternity as her eyes slowly covered every inch of the Border Collie. She felt her forehead begin to throb. Zoey had a beautiful face with the softest brown eyes that could melt the coldest iceberg of a heart.

She stood gazing up at Thea with a look of utter resignation. There was no questioning in Zoey's eyes, no hope, no happiness, and no curiosity. Zoey was accepting what had befallen her - as she always had.

Her coat was wavy and long, but very dry and painfully brittle. Bits of tar, wood chips and mud stuck to her. Behind her ears were thick mats. Zoey's long tail was a clump of felted fur as was the back of her hind legs. She looked as though she had never been brushed.

Thea dropped to her knees in front of Zoey and gently stroked the quiet Border Collie's chin. Tears began to roll down her cheeks. Zoey was thin. Zoey was very thin. Zoey was a walking skeleton. She was dangerously thin. It was obvious that Eddy had not fed Zoey in a long time.

Thea's first instinct was to grab a dog dish and fill it to the brim with food. But she couldn't do this. Zoey would die if she ate solid food. Thea led Zoey to the water dish and watched as Zoey daintily lapped up water. She lifted her head and gave Thea a brief glimmer of hope.

"Oh Zoey . . . I'm sorry I didn't get you sooner." Thea chattered to Zoey, who stood in the middle of the kitchen listening and watching. She picked up a dog dish and mixed pure maple syrup with half and half. A little bit of melted butter would be good too. She set the dish down in front of Zoey and watched as the mixture quickly disappeared. Zoey stared at Thea as though to ask for more.

"I'm sorry sweetheart. I don't think you should have anymore right now. I'm afraid for you." Thea lightly ran her hand over Zoey's head and closed her eyes to the sight of all the bones that poked out of the dog's lank body. She cut the sleeves off an old T-shirt and put it on Zoey. It was too painful to look at her thinness. It was frightening. First thing in the morning, she would take Zoey to the vet.

Thea had filled a dog crate with a thick old quilt and invited Zoey to snuggle up inside. Zoey instinctively knew it was meant for her and she curled up in the quilt, half burying her body under the comforting warmth. Within seconds, she was asleep.

Finally, after such a long time, the Border Collie was in a warm dry place. No choking car fumes in a closed garage or a hard concrete floor to lay on. This was heaven. Zoey took a deep breath and inhaled the scent of love that permeated the old quilt. She was exhausted. The walk from the car to the house had stolen all her strength.

"Thea," the vet technician said quietly as she stared at Zoey, "you should report the owner of this dog to the authorities. This is horrible. We may not be able to save this dog. She's dangerously thin."

Thea dropped to her knees and carefully wrapped her arms around Zoey. She felt a thick lump rise in her throat that she was sure had to be her heart. She felt the tears ascend within her again as she looked into Zoey's quiet brown eyes that expected and asked for nothing. Deep in the eyes, there lay a glimmer of newfound love - and this caused such incredible pain for Thea. Zoey just had to pull through this. She had to be saved!

"Do what you can for me. Please."

Zoey spent the next two days at the vet clinic and on the third day, Thea eagerly brought Zoey home. Three days of care showed no improvement in the tattered Border Collie. She was still extremely thin and weak. The only discernible difference was the look in Zoey's eyes. She was happy to see Thea. Her long thick knot of tail swung gracefully as she followed Thea out to the car.

"Here, darling," Thea whispered, "I have a nice thick sweater for you to wear." Carefully she slipped the bright red sweater over Zoey and then walked her out to the car. With instructions on how to care for Zoey, Thea took a deep breath and asked: "Will she make it?"

"I'm sorry Thea, we just don't know."

Back in the warmth of her kitchen, Thea pulled the old quilt out of the crate and bundled Zoey up in it. She sat on the floor and cradled the fragile Border Collie in her lap. There was nothing else she could do for her. Thea felt helpless.

Zoey's body grew limp as the gentle heat enveloped her. She twisted her head to look up into Thea's face. And then, the Border Collie's soft brown eyes spoke volumes.

Zoey told her she understood all this was done to help her. She appreciated the gift of the quilt, the liquid meals that did not upset her stomach. She had hungered for the kind-hearted hand like Thea's, to caress her and tell her she was deserving. She treasured the time that Thea had spent with her, talking to her. She cherished watching Thea putter around the kitchen and she enjoyed the sounds of a home filled with love. For all these things, Zoey was grateful.

Yes, this was good. Heaven is a place filled with light and warmth and love. This kitchen must be heaven. She was happier than she could remember ever having been. Zoey fixed her gentle brown eyes on Thea's face. Ever so carefully, she gave Thea a light lick on the wrist to express her profound thankfulness. It was time to rest. She nestled her head into Thea's hand and with the quietness that exemplified her temperament, Zoey released herself from the suffering that had held her to this world.

"Zoey . . . I'm so sorry. I'm so sorry . . ." Thea held the Border Collie to her bosom while she cried tears of helplessness.

For several weeks Thea felt grief envelope her like a cold scabbard. Zoey had not been with her long but she was unforgettable. It was those eyes. Those lovely eyes that had touched her. At first, Thea had felt rage toward Eddy. But Zoey's impressible eyes had taught Thea that love could endure what hatred could not. Love had patience. Calmly, Thea put her anger away, knowing it was not what Zoey would have wanted. Instead, she planted a patch of flowering herbs in the corner of the garden near Zoey's mound.

"Thea! Thea!" Beth called as she came around the corner of the farmhouse. "Where are you, girl?"

133

Thea roused from her reverie to see Beth strolling along the garden path. She smiled brightly and waved to Thea.

"Thea, honey, look what I have for you! Now, I know you've been in a blue funk since that skinny Border Collie....well, you know. But look Thea! Will you take him, hon? He's a stray that just showed up in my driveway while I was out walking my Westies. Nobody knows where he came from. I called all around. I think he was dumped. Thea, he needs your help. He's kind of skinny too - but not too skinny. Black and white too."

Thea knelt to the ground to study the Border Collie. This one was different. He had a broader head and looked like a Border Collie/Labrador Retriever mix. But his eyes. They were the same as Zoey's.

Mud and Oranges

The play area that I take Cap, Stevie and Pallie to at mid-day
had turned into a field of mud. Some idiot at city hall decided that this
bit of field needed some dirt dumped in there by the truckload.
Therefore, half the Frisbee playing area went from nice thick grass to
topsoil mixed with clay.

Then it rained. A lot. In addition, it is impossible to keep those
three Border Collies out of the mud. It also does no good to yell:

"Stay out of the mud, sweeties!"

The creek defined the east end of the play area, and heavy rains
often caused the banks to overflow every spring. For several months,
the ground remains spongy soft near the creek, and any person
weighing over ten pounds, would find water oozing up and soaking into
their shoes. It was black earth, thick with rotted leaves, smelling musty
and slightly of fish - and whatever else flowed along with current.

I stepped out of the jeep and gazed across the field. Half the
play area was an inch or so under water. The rest of the area was bare
mud. I stood there looking at the field for a few moments, wondering
how wise it would be - or not be – to let the three Border Collies out of

135

my jeep. Hm . . . perhaps I could keep them over in the wet portion only. Yes, if we walked far enough down the field, away from the muddy section...yes, this could work.

My thoughts were disrupted by the sound of the jeep's window opening. Pallie stuck her head out and barked at me:

"Well? Are you letting us out or not? The window, I can open all by myself – as you well know from this past winter. But opening the door or the hatch just isn't possible. I need thumbs for that."

I had not turned off the engine. There is a control button on the driver's side door that can lock any other window in the jeep from opening. Obviously, it was not engaged!

I shook my head. That dog! First she wants a wristwatch, then she opens and closes the windows if they are not locked. Next she's going to want to drive the jeep. Mumble, mumble, mumble.

I thought back to last winter. It was a Friday night, black as coal and bitterly cold. During the day, a sudden freezing rain had covered the earth in a thick layer of ice. The sidewalks were treacherous by the time I left work, and cautiously I slid my way down the concrete with my free hand against the buildings, back behind the building to my jeep.

"Don't pull..." I warned Pallie and KC, keenly aware of the ice beneath my feet.

I put the two dogs inside the jeep, turned the engine on and set the defrost control at full blast. I hate scraping ice off the windshield. Perhaps if I were taller and could actually reach the center of the windshield, I would feel a little differently about this.

The dogs, on the other hand, love to see me scrape the windshield. They chased the ice scraper from window to window, barking with glee and further steaming up the windows from the inside.

"Click."

Pallie stood there on the driver's seat, staring intently at the ice scraper in my hand, her paw on the door lock. Uh oh... I was locked out of the jeep with the dogs inside, engine running. All the keys to the jeep, my store, my house, were inside the jeep. Dave had gone home already.

Sigh.

"Pallie, unlock the door!"
"What's the matter, mom?" she cocked her head at me and wagged her tail happily. (Heh, heh, heh). "Time to negotiate, mom! Carpe diem! Here's a list of my demands..."

When the play session had ended, my feet were soaked. The three Border Collies had big happy smiles on their faces – and mud all over them. They had all become the same color: muddy black.

Pallie had been rolling a bright orange ball across the grassy part of the play area - and then across the muddy section. Her snowy white chest was now earth-colored. Grimy water dripped off the once white "feathers" of her belly and legs.

Stevie Ray Dog is already an earth colored dog – but his white legs were no longer white. He was now a tri-colored Border Collie: almost white, liver-colored, and black muck. He had been herding Pallie as she rolled the big orange ball across the mud. There were two things to herd here, as far as he was concerned: the big orange ball – and Pallie.

When I've had Stevie out by himself with the orange ball, his usual clumsy ways disappear. Growling and moving the ball about with the side of his face, he is just plain old fun to watch. I discovered that if I give him a stick about two feet long, he'll hold that stick in the center and use it like a rudder to steer the orange ball in a zigzag across the open field. However, if Pallie is there, he defers to her and resorts to herding and circling only.

Cap, with his long tail dragging across the mud, has spent his playtime diving after his Disc. I threw the Disc in the center of the grassy area - but he is a Border Collie with the instinct to do an outrun that just does not allow him to run out in a straight line. With the toss of the disc, Cap would cut a wide arc to the west, out to the left across the mud so he could curve back in a counterclockwise line of travel, to catch that disc. He was filthy and happy.

Pallie stood beside the jeep, looking up at me expectantly. She wanted to hop into the front passenger side seat.

"Oh no! Get in the back with Cap and Stevie Ray Dog. "

I pointed to the open hatch door and she stared at me indignant with disbelief.

"Let's negotiate, mom."

"No negotiations! Get in the back. One negotiation at a time anyways… the answer is still no to having your own wristwatch, by the way. Get in the back, Pallie."

She let out a huff and hopped in.

Twelve muddy feet are in my jeep. Wet dogs steamed up all the windows with happy hot doggie breath. The jeep needs to dry out now - but it is raining. I had to roll the windows up. I decided that it will have to be this way today – but I will have the windows rolled down all day tomorrow.

Two days later, the glorious sun comes out sending illumination and just enough warmth down to earth, to remind us that this is the tail end of summer. There is just enough warmth to warm up the interior of the jeep…just enough to encourage the development of that musty smell.

I opened the jeep door the next morning and a heavy wave of warm earthy air fell out of the jeep and spilled out onto my feet. My lungs and my nostrils collapsed. Gasp! I quickly rolled down all the windows and drove 40 mph in the 25 mph zone just so that I could get rid of that very musty smell. All day the windows remained down - but the next morning as I climbed back into my jeep, there it was again.

I went to the grocery store and spent a good twenty minutes examining all the odor control stuff. Little plug-in scent things, pull-up things, spray things, let 'em sit on the counter things, etc. Finally, I picked out a little container that I could just set on the dashboard.

Next, I seriously considered what particular scent I wanted inside my jeep. Some smells will instantly bring on asthma - like strong floral scents, burning candles, almost all perfumes, smoke.... I chose a citrus scent.

Yes, I can handle a citrus scent. Orange. This would be pleasant. I placed the little orange scent container on the dashboard and sighed with relief as the pleasant smell of oranges floated about the jeep interior.

The next morning, when I climbed into my jeep, I found that I had to roll the all the windows down again and drive 40 mph in the 25 mph zone again.

The smell hung heavy inside the jeep, and I found my asthma was flaring up. What did my jeep smell like now you ask? It smelled as though I was hauling a load of moldy, musty oranges.

Chef Cap

About an hour after mealtime, Cap came nonchalantly wandering back into the kitchen, tipping his head up toward the countertop above him. He sniffed the air for whatever molecules might come drifting down. His one prick ear followed the contour of the counter as it made a curve toward the stove. The end of his nose turned rubbery, bending to the left and then to the right. Each nostril flared slightly as he inhaled from that nostril. He paused for just a moment to process the information, and then flared the other nostril for a deep inhalation.

A dog's nasal cavity has a series of very delicate bony structures that are called tubinates. They are connected to blood and nerve supplies. Because of this, a dog's nose is extremely sensitive. The glands in the tubinates secrete a mixture of mucus and clear fluid. The olfactory nerve, which sends information to the brain, is also found in the tubinates as well as in the nasal septum, the sinuses and in parts of the bony nasal cavity.

A dog has approximately two hundred million receptors in the lining of its nose. A human has about five million receptors. Small wonder, with all those specialized cells continuous with the olfactory nerve, that a dog would have a sense of smell, said to be at least one million times more sensitive than a human nose.

Dogs do not get colds like humans do, but they do get respiratory infections. If a dog has a runny nose, it is likely due an infection, allergies, something foreign caught inside the nose, or a tumor. If there is a discharge, then it is time to go see the vet.

There was nothing caught in Cap's nose – except the stray molecules lying on the countertop. He was quite intent, like a wine connoisseur, delicately tasting the molecules as they left a message on his olfactory nerve.

"Cheese . . .dad sliced Jarlsberg cheese . . . and somebody ate peanut butter on bread. No wait . . make that wheat toast. Hm…instant coffee, oatmeal with brown sugar. (sniff sniff sniff) Cinnamon on custard . . ."

There was a momentary pause while he processed more collected molecule information in his brain. I saw his black licorice lips part ever so slightly. With sufficient data collected and now thoroughly processed, he was thinking.

"Ooo! Now here's an interesting molecule!"

Cap had forgotten I was sitting at the kitchen table, quietly working away. So typical of a Border Collie, he was deep in concentration, and he had that Border Collie "eye" fixed on what he now considered a worthwhile "job." Yes, without a job, the Border Collie will find something to do. Quick and very clever, they are, with mind ever alert and functioning. I have often said to those who seek to adopt a Border Collie:

"If you don't give them a job, they will become self-employed. And you may not like what they decide their job is going to be. As an example of self-employment: you would be surprised how much wicker goes into making a wicker chair!"

Light as a feather, Cap stood on his hind feet and gently placed his front paws on the edge of the counter - to get a better look. Slowly, he tilted his head sideways to get his nose closer to the molecules that must have been lying dormant on the countertop. Just about that time, I saw his lips open wider and out came his tongue.

"Cap, off," I whispered.

Cap's ears folded back behind him, aimed in my direction, and he slowly pushed himself off the counter to drop his front feet back on the floor. With the same easy-going attitude, he sauntered a few steps in my direction, flashing his white teeth in a big grin.

"I was just checking, mom." His tail fluttered, and mumbling to himself, he left the room.

"Humans. They leave molecules all over the counter – and then wipe them off with that wet dishtowel instead of letting a dog take care of them. You'd never catch me leaving molecules behind. I belong to the Clean Dog Dish club . . ."

I called him back, and he leaned against my legs as though nothing mischievous had ever entered his head. He looked up at me adoringly and gave me another sweet little smile.

"We've had this discussion many times, Cap," I said.

He gave me a sideways glance and his eyes quickly shifted to the countertop, then back to me. Yes, he knew what I was talking about. I swear he reads my mind at times.

"Stay off the counter. If you're going be checking out the countertop, you better be making dinner for everybody."

I suspect he checks out the countertop while I am at work - but I do not know this for sure since nothing is ever disturbed when I get home, and I do not have the olfactory abilities that he does. I smiled to myself, thinking that would truly be an amazing job, though, to teach him to make dinner.

"What d'ya say, Cap? Since you seem to know the countertop so well, want to make dinner for everybody tomorrow evening?" I stroked down the length of his body as he leaned against me.

"Yeah. Sure," said Cap. " I can do dinner. Is that all you want? I can flip kibble into a bowl for you."

The Old Dog

"Twelve-year-old female Border Collie. Her time is nearly up. Very loving, gives kisses freely. Somebody please help this dog."

I read that and it got to me. For what reason did a loving, twelve-year-old Border Collie end up in a shelter? Well . . . (sigh). It wasn't something that I could concentrate on because we could not take the dog into our rescue. We had no room. As usual, there is no room.

I shook my head sadly but did not delete the post. She was a long way from here. Maybe there was a rescuer nearer that would take her - or she would be adopted . . . but she was twelve years old. It can be very hard to find a home for a dog that old - and there are a lot of younger ones who need our help just as badly, and would be easier to place. We would probably have her for a long time while others were put down waiting to come into rescue. But it's not her fault she's twelve and ended up in a shelter. Age should not be a penalty.

I turned my computer off. I could not think about it. We had no room for another dog - of any age right now. Instead, I searched for ways to take this dog into rescue; to find someone who could help but met without success.

It is estimated that seven to twelve million dogs pass through animals shelters each year. The majority do not find a new home and are euthanized. The pet overpopulation problem is large, and humane societies all across the nation struggle with educating the public while taking in their pets. Funding to keep a humane society might be supported by the local government, but often times it is not.

Breed rescue organizations are typically full and there is a waiting list to get a dog into the rescue. It is a wonderful way to rehome a dog, but it means thinking ahead, being patient, and staying in contact with the rescue organization until an opening is available.

A good rescue organization will work with the family who seeks to rehome their dog. They may offer training help, behavior modification advice, or suggest other alternatives to help a family keep their dog.

That night an old dog that I had never met ruined my sleep. In my dreams, I saw a slightly heavy-bodied but quiet and gentle dog, sitting in the middle of a gray concrete floor surrounded by a woven wire kennel. All around her were anxious, stressed dogs that paced, panted and barked for somebody to come and get them.

The old Border Collie sat there quietly trying to shut out the sounds and motion about her. Her tired head hung a bit low. In my sleep, she looked at my soul with patient eyes and spoke to me.

"Please ...come."

We had no room - and I pushed this dog out of my mind for a week as I kept busy with other aspects of the rescue, but still looked for ways to get this old dog out of the shelter. When night came and I fell asleep, the old dog was there sitting quietly in the kennel, waiting for me to fall asleep.

"Please ...come."

In the second week another message appeared on my computer.

"Very sweet and loving Border Collie. Gives kisses freely. Please somebody save her. She deserves better than to spent her last days in a shelter."

I was beginning to dread going to bed because the old dog would be there waiting for me, staring at me...would not leave me alone. I tossed and turned in my warm and comfortable bed, and the old dog lay down on the hard concrete floor panting lightly; watching me in my dreams as I slept.

"Please ... come."

"We have no room for you, old one."

"Yes you do. I will stay at your home. I am a good dog. I won't cause trouble. Please ... come."

"You're very far away and I work every day. I can not come to get you, old one."

"Send someone. I am very good in the car. Please come for me."

"My husband doesn't want another foster dog in the house."

"He will like me. I am a good dog. You'll see. Please ... come get me."

"OK. I will talk to him."

"So will I."

By chance, Melissa ended up driving down to pick up two dogs, and was destined to pass very near the shelter where the old Border Collie waited. On her way back, she stopped at the shelter and brought the old one with her.

"I got the old dog - and guess what. She's a he! He's very sweet and loving. He rides extremely well in the car. He sat there with his head on my shoulder nearly the whole way, wanting to be petted. You should see all the ticking on his feet. Can you pick him up from my house after work?"

He had no collar, no leash, and no identification. He was a stray. He walked into my house, looked around, and smiled up at me as though he knew me. A slow patient wag of the tail and that gentle smile told me he was happy to be here. His amber eyes were sunken into his head and they looked like the eyes of a dog that had been stressed for a long time. He was tired and he desperately needed to sleep. I led him to the crate that would be his and he understood. Without a sound, he walked into the crate, circled twice and laid down to rest. It was the first time in many weeks he would be sleeping on a thick wool blanket and in a quiet place. The amber eyes disappeared behind heavy eyelids in peaceful sleep.

And I slept peacefully too.

Old Dog was still tired the next morning but he greeted me with tail thumping against the side of his crate. For a brief instant, a look of uncertainty passed over his face. The tail slowed and his head dropped just slightly. He was waiting for a response from me.

"Hi Old Dog!" I whispered and smiled. "And did you sleep well last night?'

Thump thump thump. He let out a small sigh of relief. He had not misjudged.

"I'm sorry to have to tell you this fella, but you have to go to the vet today. There are no records of any kind on you, and you will have to have all your vaccinations. You'll get a physical exam and a microchip too. I'm glad that you don't have kennel cough or fleas."

A careful observation is necessary when a new dog comes into rescue. The first thing I do is take a good look at the records that came with the dog. Sometimes there is very little. Other times, there is a complete history, which includes the dog's pedigree.

I inspected Old Dog's paperwork to see if vaccinations were current, and also to see how thorough it was. Was a heartworm check done? How about a fecal check? Has the dog been spayed or neutered? Is there any suggestion of other physical problems? If anything is missing, then an appointment to the vet needs to be made. After reviewing the papers, I do a physical exam, looking for signs of infection, fleas or worms, lameness and injuries.

I stepped back and looked at the old dog. He stood patiently still, not intent on exploring this new place. He seemed to understand that I was inspecting him. He turned slightly to show me the length of his body and looked up at me again. Hmmm...he has done this before. Old Dog had a beautiful coat. It was healthy and free of mats. His nails had been cared for, his ears were clean, his teeth were just slightly in need of cleaning, and his body weight was perfect for him. He appeared to be in excellent health. I marveled that this old dog would allow me to handle him without the slightest bit of nervousness on his part. He actually seemed to enjoy the inspection. He was used to being fussed over. Somebody had taken very good care of this old dog - and then he had ended up in the shelter.

"What happened to you, Old Dog?"

Old Dog immediately fit in. He behaved as if he had been in my house all his life. Obviously, he was not a dog that had been tied to a tree or doghouse in the backyard. He was house trained and crate trained. He was polite and attentive.

I dug into the "dog drawer" and pulled out KC's light blue collar. It was the first collar that I had put on him when he had arrived at my house as an emaciated stray with dry brittle fur. The worry on KC's face and his desperate need to be held and loved, had melted my heart. KC had loved this blue collar.

When I would remove it from him, he would slink and cower as he sought to find a safe corner. However, when the collar was on him again, his fears vanished. Eventually, when KC had overcome this fear, I had replaced the blue collar for a lovely dark red woven one as a symbol of his success. The old blue collar reminded me of "the before days."

I stood with the light blue collar in my hand, gentle rotating it and feeling every surface of the closed loop. Closing my eyes, I remembered the trip to the veterinary hospital when KC had his total hip replacement.   This light blue collar had been removed and KC thought I had taken him to a shelter.   He thought I didn't love him enough to keep him. I remembered my heart breaking for him because I couldn't explain to him that I would be coming back in a few days to get him again after his surgery. He had turned his head away sadly and wouldn't look at me anymore. I had cried on the way home, feeling sorry for KC. But the joy on his face when I pulled the collar from my pocket on the day I picked him up!

And now the collar was once again in my hand. I was about to put it on another stray - another dog with no name. When Old Dog would eventually leave my home to live with his new owners, he would be wearing this light blue collar - and it was possible that I would never see this old dog or the blue collar again.

I was torn about putting it on him. The collar represented a lot of patient love, and the struggles that KC had to overcome. It was a blue badge that spoke to me of courage and hope, and of winning KC's trust. Should I run down to the store and buy a different collar for this old dog?... no. KC didn't need this collar anymore. He would never wear it again. And Old Dog had nothing to wear.

I held the collar out to Old Dog. He understood, stretched his head out to receive it, and a happy smile spread over his face.   All the while that I had stood there thinking about giving it to him, he had been silently sitting in front of me, watching me and hoping that I would. He wanted to wear the collar! He wanted to belong to somebody again.

Do you have to go outside?" Old Dog trotted to the back door and waited for me to open it. Somebody had spent time talking to this dog. He knew a routine. I hooked a leash to him and we went out for a walk. Old Dog stepped hesitantly at first. Where was I taking him? Was I taking him away?

"Heel."

A look of confidence returned and Old Dog put his head up proudly. It had been awhile since he had heard that word. However, he understood what it meant and he walked gracefully by my side. It was good to hear familiar words again.

Somebody had trained this dog well - and then he had ended up in a shelter.

"**Tip**.....Sam.....Jack.....Fido.....Ring.....Buster.....Sky.....Ben.....Mac......Doone.....ahhh....Al.....Bob?"

Nothing. The Old Dog walked along beside me with his ears nearly touching at the back of his head. He wore a large smile on his face and was very intend on heeling. The happiness radiated from him. How wonderful to be away from the shelter and out for a lovely walk. Old Dog ignored the passing cars, running kids and bicycles. His ears pricked as a squirrel raced up a tree - but Old Dog knew to stay with me. He smiled:

"Did you see it?"

"Yes, Old Dog. I saw the squirrel. You're such a good boy, aren't you."

He wagged his tail. Each time I told him he was a good boy, a sad kind of happiness crossed his face. He had heard these words before. Was he remembering someone else?

152

"Mike.....Spot....Fee....Bart....Bear....Jim....Pi....Ajax....Ralph....Bill....
Max....Blackie....Homer.....?"

Still nothing. Nearly 100 names later, I still hadn't stumbled onto the Old Dog's name. He would stand there smiling at me, knowing that I was talking to him. It was as though he was saying:

"Nope. That's not it. Nope, that isn't it either."

I finally gave up and decided to call him Murphy. But the Old Dog didn't care for the name. I spent the next three days trying to teach him a new name but Old Dog would have nothing to do with Murphy. I could not let him off his leash because he was unaware that I was speaking to him unless he was looking directly at me. For a brief instant, I considered the possibility that he was deaf. But no, he could hear the kibble falling into his dish.

Each evening, the Old Dog would become restless. He sat very still before me and would lay a paw on my lap. What was he trying to tell me? All his needs had been met - except for that one big need.

He wanted his owner to come and get him. Old Dog would pant and stare keenly at me. He would nudge my hand and smile at me. He would lay his head in my hands and look at me in the most pitiful manner. What did Old Dog want? What was he trying to tell me? I wished that I could read his mind or that we could speak the same language.

I was compelled to drop to my knees. I held my hands out to Old Dog and he walked into my arms. He buried his face against my neck and let out a sigh. I could feel his head grow heavy as his whole body became very still and relaxed. Old Dog had wanted to be cuddled. He wanted somebody to hold him. For the longest time he stood leaning into me with his head tight to my cheek. I heard the sadness in each breath.

If a dog can cry quietly, Old Dog had finally gotten to the place where he was mourning his loses. He wanted comforting and someone to hold him while he mourned. Old Dog understood he was never going to see his master again.

I held him tight and gently patted his side. It seemed to help. Finally, he looked up at me with his sober amber colored eyes and gave me one of his kisses. His eyes were trying to tell me something, and it was an important thing he wanted me to know - but I could not understand what he was saying to me.

"Old Dog . . . I'm sorry."

"Grace. Its Melissa," the voice said over the phone. "Lois has decided she would like to adopt the old dog. But she wants to know if we would be willing to meet her halfway. I can take Murphy and meet her. I know you have to work, and I don't mind making the trip with Murphy."

"Thanks Melissa, but I think that I would like to make the trip. Lois might have some questions about Murphy and since he's been with me, I think I would be easiest for me to answer them for her."

I looked down at Old Dog and suddenly felt depressed. Old Dog was being adopted. Why did I feel so sad about it? I should be happy for Old Dog. He would finally have a place of his own again.

I spent the evening getting all his papers ready. I brushed him out and trimmed his dewclaws. Then we cuddled and Old Dog got his tummy rub. Old Dog thoroughly enjoyed the quiet time together without realizing that this was my way of saying good-bye to him.

Tomorrow we would be taking the long trip to meet Lois. But tonight he was my old dog for the last time. All mine. Tonight I would say good-bye because tomorrow it would be impossible to say it without my heart breaking into little pieces. Looking into Old Dog's gentle eyes, I realized that an old dog was a wonderful thing.

"Old Dog, this is our last day together."

I had difficulty sleeping . . . strange dreams about walking down the sidewalk in an unknown city with Old Dog on a leash beside me.

As I looked down at Old Dog, I noticed that my legs had become not my legs but that of a man wearing black jeans. And my shoes were men's shoes.

As my hand swung by, it was a man's hand. My hand swung over the Old Dog's head to pet him lovingly, and Old Dog looked up at me with bright happiness.

"Good boy . . . you're a good boy," the voice softly whispered to Old Dog. It wasn't my voice but a man's voice.

"I'm your good boy, master. I love you. Where have you been, master? I've been waiting for you." Old Dog spoke in my dreams.

His eyes sparkled with happiness and he lightly pranced with the joy that traveled down to his feet. He could not take his eyes off me as we walked along. He was so happy.

"Good boy . . . you're my good boy."

My hand reached out to caress Old Dog's head again - but this time it was my own hand. Old Dog looked up at me startled and he sat down suddenly to stare at me.

"Where did he go?!" Old Dog asked me.

"I don't know, Old Dog. I never saw him . . . I'm sorry Old Dog."

Old Dog's head dropped and he slowly exhaled. He rose to his feet like an old dog. His joy had evaporated.

"I am dreaming . . ." Old Dog said.

"So am I, Old Dog."

That morning, after a lot of fussing around, I hooked Old Dog to a leash and opened the car door. Pallie squeezed out the back door and jumped into the car before I could tell her "no." Ah well...it might be a very good thing for me to have her with me.

Old Dog jumped into the jeep also. He was all smiles. I'm sure he thought we were going out to walk the wooded trails again. But the jeep went in the opposite direction and we left town, headed north... way north.

Pallie settled herself comfortably in the front seat, and seeing how relaxed Pallie was, the Old Dog settled down too. After an hour, he became restless. The distance was too far. Something was different today. The last time he had taken a long drive like this, he had ended up as a stranger in my house. Old Dog laid his head on my shoulder and I reached up to reassure him.

"Yes, we are now a very long way away from your home. But we have found a new home for you, dear. I hope you will be very happy."

By the time I reached our destination, my lower back was fatigued from sitting. I pulled into the parking lot of Burger King and a woman in a dark pink coat called out to me. It was Lois. She looked very alert and slightly nervous. Her eyes darted over to my jeep.

"Hi Lois! Did you just get here?"

". . . well, no. I was so excited, that we left kind of early and I guess we've been waiting for quite awhile." She smiled and glanced back at her sister who followed her to my jeep. Lois pointed to my jeep where Pallie stood looking out the back at us.

"Ohh! Look! He's such a beautiful dog! Ohh . . ."

Old Dog had repositioned himself behind the steering wheel.

"Murphy is sitting in the driver's seat. He drove us here this morning. He's such a smart fella."

"Ohh . . ." Lois crooned as she peered through the jeep window at Old Dog,"He's so cute! Ohhhh . . . just look at him. I love him already."

I opened the door and Old Dog calmly hopped out of the jeep. He looked up at Lois and gave her his smile. Lois reached down to him and he lightly licked her fingers. After a few minutes, I put Pallie and Old Dog back into the jeep and we went inside to take care of all the paperwork. I gave Lois all the necessary information that she would need to know.

"Lois, I have no puppy pictures to give you of Murphy. The very best that I can do is tell you how it is that he came to be with me. It was a little paragraph in my email that said 'Gives kisses freely' that got to me and because of it, Murphy will be your dog. Please love him and take care of him like the very special dog that he is."

With paperwork completed, we walked back to the jeep and I let Old Dog out once again. I knelt on the cold pavement and opened my arms to him. He smiled at me and walked into my arms, snuggled his head against my neck as I held him tight. How soft and warm his fur is. He stood very still except for the wide swinging of his tail, and he drank in the warm feelings and my love that I was sending along with him. I released him and he backed up a step to gaze into my face. He knew. His eyes were quiet and accepting. He knew this was good-bye.

"You're a good boy. Make me proud of you," I whispered ever so quietly into his silky soft ear. "Don't forget me . . . and once in awhile, when you and I are sleeping, come visit me again. Good-bye Old Dog."

Lois opened her car door for Old Dog. He looked back at me one last time and our eyes met once more. He understood, and it was OK with him.

Old Dog quietly hopped into the car, and the door closed.

Trick 'r Treat

Tis the dreaded Halloween time. I don't know how the rest of you feel - but my Border Collies are convinced that this is the most evil night of the year. Oh yes, for sure the Fourth of July is also a nasty night – but Halloween is by far the most evil.

Here they are minding their own doggie business when suddenly the doorbell rings! They all rush to the door, tails held high with excitement, barking their fool heads off until I remind them they are using their outside voices.

"It's the pizza dude! It's the pizza dude! Woo Hoo!!"

Prancing on hind feet, with strings of saliva already swinging like the pendulum of a grandfather clock, the dogs dance about as visions of pepperoni floated through their heads. Woo Hoo!! Already their noses were busy searching for the scent of warm pizza.

I shuffled through the dogs and cautiously open the door. Bathed in the pallid horror lighting of the lone porch light, a small red satin goblin stared up at me. He had a hideous snarl painted wildly on his little face. One horn was tipped backward rakishly.

"Tricker Treat! Tricker Treat!!"

159

He thrust a bright orange plastic pumpkin at me, partially filled with candies and twisted his garish mouth into a most gruesome and toothless grin.
I peered inside the plastic pumpkin, curious to know what the neighbors were handing out. Huh. Someone is giving out small apples.

I remember as a child out doing the "Trick r Treat Route," getting annoyed when I would get an apple. This is not the time to be thinking healthy stuff. Its junk food time! Sweet stuff! Tooth-rotting stuff!

An apple?

I would politely thank the giver and then, in the cover of the darkness- far enough away from the house that no one would see - pitch that apple as far as I could toss it and then listen for the dull thud as it hit the ground somewhere out there in the blackness. Oh yes. Get rid of the apple.

"Apples are good for you, you know," my older sister would say as she studied her apple.

"There's another here in my bag. Do you want it?" I pulled the apple out of my bag and held it out to her.

"Um . . . no thank you. I have two already. Besides, mom and dad will wonder why I have three and you have none. I'm sure they would make me share the apples with you – and you'd get your apple back anyway."

160

Sigh.

"You could throw your apples away too . . ."
"No . . . then mom and dad would think it odd that we didn't get any apples this year.   We'd get the Spanish Inquisition until we confessed. And he would squeal on us anyway."   She pointed to our darling little brother.

Sigh.

Mom would always inspect our goodies when we got home and if there was an apple in there, she would make us eat that before we could eat anything else in our hard-earned pile of sweets.
And heaven forbid if there were two apples in there! Who had room for candy after having to eat two apples?! Sometimes I would barely manage a piece of candy after the two apples, and later I would have a tummy ache. Mom would declare that I had eaten too many sweets. No . . . it was from eating those blasted apples!

I dropped two little chocolate candy bars into the plastic pumpkin. Yes, we give out the good stuff at our house . . . cuz if there's candy left over, it had better be something that I want to eat. Chocolate. The nectar of the gods. Soul food. Happiness wrapped in foil.
"Wow!" said the little red goblin. "Good stuff! Thanks!"
Cap had followed me to the door, being the bold little fella that he is. He balanced effortlessly on his hind feet, lightly touching the screen door with one front paw. His one merle ear ricocheted forward. He froze.

"Oh m'god! What the hell is that?! . . . Its a red . . . what the hell IS that?!! Intruder! Intruder! Introooder! Where's the pizza dude?! The little red thing musta got him. Introoder!"

Cap dashed back and forth alerting the other three dogs. All the dogs had to pile up at the door, deeply suspicious now. With good cause too, because looming out there on the sidewalk just beyond the porch light, were two large hulking figures standing there with their hideous hands stuffed in their pockets, and their heads low against the damp wind. Obviously, these are the creators of this little red goblin that took down the pizza dude.

Cap sniffed the air.

"Kind of smells like a kid." He bristled. Cap hated kids. "Enough to give a dog the hives . . ." It was an ugly little red thing.

"Smells like a kid . . ."

Across the street and bouncing along from house to house, small tight beams from flashlights moved through the darkness. The muffled sound of leaves being trampled and shuffled through reached four sets of doggie ears.

Silhouettes of never before seen shapes appeared and disappeared before the neighbors' windows.

Stevie Ray Dog held his ears as high as he could - which was just slightly higher than parallel to the floor. His pupils grew large and dark as he nervously watched in alarm. Creatures of all sorts were surrounding the house, coming up the sidewalk, crossing HIS front lawn. Monsters. They were everywhere!! The doorbell rang again.

"WOO WOO WOO!!!"

I put all the dogs in their crates. Thank God it is only one night a year.

Later, when all was quiet again and the witching hour was done and gone, I let the dogs out. Stiffed-legged they crept through the house, still leery. Did she let any of those critters in the house? They checked out the dark corners, the closets, and the place where the dog food is kept. (Oh good . . . the food is still safe).

"Where's the pizza dude?" they wanted to know. KC ran to the living room window and peered out at the night, scanning the ground for a pizza box. No pizza box. The monsters must have dragged the pizza box off with them too. All is lost. He was a good man, that pizza dude.

By the end of the evening, the remainder of the chocolate sat in a small box at the very center of the dining room table. Two unopened bags. Cool. Stevie Ray Dog sat down facing the table, thinking to himself. No pizza . . . just those two bags that mom is trying to hide up there on the table . . .

The next morning, before heading off to work, I walked about the yard, picking up dropped candies and wrappers. Somebody must have had a hole in his or her bag. And, there on the ground amidst the maple leaves, sat a small apple. Huh.

It was around 2:00 in the afternoon when I came home to let the dogs out. I put Cap in the jeep and we drove off to the open field for a bit of disc catching.

A Perfectly Good Dog

It was just a little bit on the warm side, but there was a strong wind coming from across the lake. I tossed the disc up the hill and Cap chased after it happily. He would only be able to do this for about 15 minutes before his body would overheat.

Cap has a condition called Malignant Hyperthermia. Although many dogs will overheat, this is something just a little bit different. Apparently, calcium builds up in the muscles and causes the overheating problem. A dog with Malignant Hyperthermia will overheat in just minutes, regardless of what the outside temperature is.

A normal temperature for a dog is 101-102 degrees. After fifteen minutes of exercise, on a cold day, Cap's body temperature can rise to 107 degrees, which is dangerously high and can result in seizures, damaged organs and death. A vet will test for Malignant Hyperthermia but taking a core sample of muscle tissue and checking the mineral content. A layman can do a simple test by taking the body temperature, exercise the dog for ten minutes, and recheck the body temperature.

It is genetic, rare, and there is no cure for it. The only thing that can be done is managing the amount of exercise, and making a diet change.

I watched Cap carefully and when that look started to come over his face, he began to pant more heavily. We quit and I took him back home.

He threw himself on the deck, slightly stiff-legged again, leaning and struggling to keep his balance. I sat down on the deck and watched him closely to see if I needed to do something else. In a few minutes, he had mostly recovered. I carried him inside and set him in the doggie bath tub to slowly cool him down. I shook my had sadly and lightly stroked Cap's head.

"I'm sorry, little fella. That was only seven minutes of tossing the disc, and you were done. I thought you'd get a little more play time today, what with the weather being cooler."

I carried Cap up the stairs and set him down. Stevie Ray Dog came sauntering in the room with the biggest smile on his face, happily chewing on something. He wagged his tail with delight in knowing that we had returned. He headed for the door. He wanted to be outside. But first: a drink of water.

I glanced back into the dining room, and there spread out on the floor was a collection of foil wrappers. They were soggy, chewed and flat. On the dining room table sat two more wrappers. The small box was tipped over and one bag of chocolates was pulled slightly toward the edge of the table, ripped open.

Stevie has never put his paws on the dining room table. Today was a first. I hooked him up to a lead and let him out into the backyard. Then I called the vet.

"How much did he eat?"

"The bag says it contains a pound and seven ounces of chocolate. Half the bag is missing."

Stevie Ray Dog happily jumped into the jeep, unaware that he was going to visit the vet. I left him there for the afternoon while they induced vomiting and poured liquid charcoal down his throat.

He was a very unhappily looking dog at 6:00 in the evening when I picked him up again. His chin was black with charcoal, the bottom of one foot was black, and he had the saddest eyes you're going to see on a chocolate-loving dog.

Quietly he entered the house and crawled over to a corner, eyeing me as though he had done something really bad. His ears remained flat to his skull for the rest of the evening.

"Poor Stevie," I said softly to him.

He scurried over to me and laid his head in my lap.

"Them is my chocolates. You mess with my chocolates, and you'll regret it. Poor Stevie."

He tucked his head into my hands, obviously sorry. Stevie let out a sigh and looked up at me sadly.

"No chocolates . . . and no pizza dude either."

A Toss of the Disc

It seemed like just a few days earlier, the temperature had been ten degrees below zero and I had bundled up in a sweatshirt, two jackets, and a pair of light earmuffs under my hood and lined wind pants over my jeans. My thick felt-lined boots kept my feet warm - but the bitterly cold wind had frozen my forehead so numb that I worried my frontal lobe might freeze to the inside of my skull. It was the beginning days of March, and winter had grown quite tiresome. The snow was old and dirty, and with the frequent freeze/thaw cycles, well, you could hardly call it "snow" anymore.

Months of gray, overcast skies and dead grass protruding stiffly through chunks of dirty ice, coming home from work when the sun had long ago set behind the black silhouettes of the Norfolk pines, I longed for spring. The freeze/thaw cycles were teasers. Yes, spring was here. No ... no, it isn't. Wait. Here it comes again! Snow flurries, ice storms, and brilliant days sent the daily temperatures first soaring – and then plunging. Many of us "northerners" begin to suffer cabin fever at this time of the year.

As usually happens, spring finally arrived abruptly in a flurry of activity. High winds from the south blow the last of the cold and ice away, and small rivers form along the roadsides. The creek had once again overflowed its banks, which caused marshes to form in the adjoining fields. Thousands of frogs lay hidden amidst the thick grass, warmed by the sun and hidden except for the cacophony of their sound.

I got out the orange Disc and twirled it between my fingers while I considered where to take Cap today. The ground was very soft - nay, it was muddy. Even Cap's light body was heavy enough to sink an inch into the soil as he trotted across the lawn. I thought about the little park where we usually went to play and considered what it probably looked like. The gravel parking lot would be half under water...but it was still the best place to take Cap. It was far enough away from traffic, no other dogs around, there was a creek for him to jump in to cool off and an area large enough to toss a Disc.

The little park sits on the edge of town, nearly invisible and virtually ignored. Someone comes out to mow the grass near the parking area, and once a month the city crew will empty the green fifty-five gallon barrel that holds the garbage. This little park had at one time been a farm and the concrete foundation of the barn still defines the size of what was once the barn.

I had often wondered what this homestead had looked like back in the days when our town had been a bustling hub. The barn had sat tight to the slope of the creek that ran north and south. It had been a large barn. I could imagine this place as it might have been a hundred years ago. I would have spent my summers out by the barn, had I been a child back then. With a book in hand, I would have kicked off my shoes somewhere in the dark shadows of the dusty barn...perhaps up in the hayloft. I would have sat down on one of the large erratic limestone rocks along the bank – or climbed out onto an overhanging willow bough. I would have enjoyed the pleasure of a good book in the quiet shade behind the barn, invisible from the rest of the world.

The endless background music would have been the sounds of the creek and the ducks, thinly written like a Liszt piano concerto yet filled with the complexities of tonalities and rhythmic oddities only God can write.

A hundred years have passed, but I imagine that some things remain the same. The sun still shines bright, and the mornings are still hazy and filled with the musty earthy smells. The dragonflies still skim over the slow moving creek and large lazy catfish still scour the muddy bottom. The water still overflows its banks each spring. The land between the creek and the cottonwood trees still becomes the home to red-winged blackbirds, muskrats, water snakes and frogs. Sandhill cranes still echo their rasping sounds from the opposite bank, hidden high in the tangled branches of trees. Things change ... but things stay the same... stay the same.

I called Cap and he raced to the back of my open jeep and hopped in. His eyes were bright with happiness because he had seen the Disc. He knew where we were going: to his private little park by the creek. His lower jaw quivered with anticipation and he sat as tall as he could, staring intently ahead.

I had long ago learned to keep the jeep windows closed when Cap was inside but not in his crate. On numerous occasions, he had tossed his Disc out the window with me unaware of it until we had arrived at the park – with no Disc anywhere in the jeep. We would have to back track until we came upon the Disc lying in the middle of the road.

Yes indeed. The little gravel parking lot had turned into a large puddle that looked like creamed coffee. Cap whined most pitifully as the jeep slowed down. His eyes focused on the field beyond the circular parking lot, already picking the line he would run just as soon as his feet hit the ground. He was anxious to play.

169

I opened the jeep door and before I could swing my legs out or even turn my body to stand up, Cap squeezed out the door behind me. He dashed off with a splash as his feet hit the large puddle, drenching his clean white fur to a soggy gray. He soared over the parking barrier as though it were not there and glanced over his shoulder at the same time.

Cap ran a wide outrun, circled the edge of the mowed clearing and kept the eye on the white side of his face intent on me with a look that unmistakably said:

"Throw it!"

Cap streaked across the open field and flew gracefully toward the clouds to meet his Disc. I thought about all those other things he could be doing. His previous owners, were no doubt, exasperated by his boundless energy and numerous fears.

Before Cap had reached adulthood, they had come to realize that this beautiful Border Collie was too much for them to live with, too difficult to understand and needed far more exercise than they were willing to commit to on a daily basis. Exasperated, impatient and an unable to maintain a gentle spirit with such a dog, they decided they needed to move Cap out of their house. Out – anywhere – just out of their house and out of their lives.

I spoke to an animal communicator about him. Cap told her that he did not like children. He especially did not like them coming at him. They are mean, he said. They chased him and threw things at him. No, he does not like kids.

Cap arrived a bundle of nerves and pent up energy with no outlet. He was also a little too skinny. He is an unusually patterned Border Collie. He has a half mask, meaning the left side of his face is black while the other side is white. His black ear has silver splotches and folds outward and to the side in what is called a rose fold. The right ear stands bolt upright and is merled in blacks and grays. He wears a wide band of white fur that covers his shoulders, and his front legs are spotted like a Dalmatian. He looks like a committee designed him.

During the first six months in our home Cap paced, circled, and barked. The pads of his feet were constantly damp from stress and he left little wet paw prints on the tile flooring. He was ever vigilant, insecure, and worried about what would happen next. At that time, the only things he could focus on – besides moving cars – were tennis balls or his flying Disc. I quickly learned that correcting him increased his anxiety and caused his behavior to worsen. Finally, after three months of trying many different approaches with him and seeing little progress, I suddenly changed his name to Cap one morning.

The affect was dramatic. It was as though I had touched the "off button." Initially, Cap was confused. I had stopped calling him by his old name and now he did not know to whom I was talking. He would look over his shoulder to see if there was another dog standing behind him, and then look at me again with his head cocked. Instead of pacing about restlessly or barking, he would lay down quietly to think about this new word he was hearing.

He figured it out on the second day.

"Cap, come," and I held out my hands to me while squatting on the floor.

Suddenly his merle ear popped forward and a big smile spread rapidly across his beautiful face. The tail flickered happily and he trotted over to me to take his treat.

"Oh!" he seemed to say. "I understand now! You're talking to me. I'm Cap!"

The progression of events that had always followed his name was erased. Previously, someone would call his name, tell him to come, and then over-correct him when he came. By changing his name, the whole progression had crumbled and now, Cap was delighted to come when called. Coming when called by the old name meant a correction of some sort – but coming when called "Cap" meant a treat, loving and playtime. It was a much better thing to be "Cap."

Gradually, Cap's memory of his previous name disappeared and with it went the wild and uncontrollable spirit, the constantly damp feet, and the unwillingness to be touched. Cap became eager to please, learned quickly, and looked to me for comfort or reassurance that he was indeed, safe. Instead of avoiding being touched, he leaned against my legs to wait for the long strokes down his back and a massage.

Cap flourished in all positive training. I had learned over the first six months that he was a very "soft" dog and a harsh word was enough to hurt his feelings. He needed to succeed and more than anything, he needed to know that no matter what, I would always be there to keep harm away.

When he had finally learned to trust me, he was then able to learn other things. I took him to an obedience class on the fifth week of the class. Not expecting him to learn, as he was already far behind the rest of the class, Cap surprised me by catching up to the rest of the class in fifteen minutes. Like a cat, he learned from watching.

I decided to teach him some cute little tricks after that and his best is called "Be healed." Like a faith healer, Cap will place a paw on my arm, fold his ears down and bow his head with his eyes closed.

"Amen." Cap will spring back into action with a happy smile on his face.

Cap floated effortlessly over the grass with his tail flowing out behind him, motionless. He ran silently with speed, power and such marvelous coordination and focus. He is a superb athlete and knows exactly where his body is in time and space. Such beauty to behold, such freedom. I wish I could move like that....

I smiled to myself and took his favorite orange Disc out of the jeep. Cap circled the edge of the clearing, watching me. Even from this distance, I could see his face grow serious, his eyes grow dark with anticipation, and the tension in his muscles explodes in a burst of speed.

What is it that makes the way he runs so utterly beautiful to watch? I never tire of studying him. Eventually he with lay down at my feet with his tattered Disc between his front paws, breathless but still chewing the Disc because his heart says he loves this day and his body says "not another step." I feel all the love in the world for him. What a joy to know him. What an honor to have his trust and his smile.

"Throw it!"

He ran a wide arc across the field and cut to the east because I had turned my shoulder ever so slightly. He knew which way the Disc would travel. With his head parallel to the ground, he cast quick glances in my direction, and ran. Often I throw the Disc far enough out that it isn't possible for Cap to reach it in time - because I love to see him run and scoop up the Disc in one continuously fluid motion. He doesn't mind a bit. It is not the catch that is important. Obviously, there must be something else about Discs that he enjoys so much. After one hundred tosses, my aim began to get sloppy and Cap had to work a little harder to make some wild catches.

"Throw it!"

I threw the Disc – and watched as the wind plucked it from the course I had set for it and flicked it high over the tall swamp grass. It turned slightly on its side and flew to the left - right into the marsh where the grass was eight feet tall and very thick.

Cap ran along beneath the Disc with his head tipped toward the sky. He sliced through the tall grass and disappeared. All I heard was the rustling and the splashing sounds as he wandered about looking for his Disc. Five minutes later, he parted the tall green curtain of marshy grass and stepped onto the mowed section - all wet. No Disc. He scanned my hands to see if I had thought to bring another Disc out to play. Nope.

The look on his sweet face told a whole story all by itself. It was somewhere between worry for his Disc and hope that I knew where it was. He was speaking to me, sending me his thoughts so very clearly that they were almost audible.

"You throw like a left-handed girl!"

I was not about to wade into the dense grass and water to find Cap's Disc. I loaded a very disappointed – and probably disgusted Cap back into the jeep. Our Disc session was done for the day.

The following day was equally beautiful but a bit windy. I let Cap out of the jeep and he took off like a shot, heading for the far side of the clearing with the expectation that his Disc would sail over his shoulder.

Sploosh!

Sigh . . .

Cap stood his ground. This time he did not go charging through the thick wall of marsh grass after his brand new pink Disc. He rolled his eyes at me and turned his head away in an obvious display of disgust.

(She did it again. Another stupid toss! Let's see . . . how many is that now . . .) Cap stared at his front feet for a moment, deep in thought, counting his toes.

I was hoping that he couldn't count above the number four - because that's how many times I had tossed this new Disc before it kind of stuck to my thumb and took that wild left hook high into the sky where the wind caught it . . . and then it disappeared waaay out there in the marsh.

". . . Um . . . go get the Disc, Cap!" I said to him with as much enthusiasm as I could fake.

He turned his head toward the marsh, remembering yesterday, and then slowly looked back at me. (Have you ever had a Border Collie look at you like that? You know, like they sort of suspect that they might possibly be smarter than you?)

Cap turned toward the marsh and just stood there with the black curls of his butt facing me. His tail hung most unenthusiastically.

(Oh yea . . . make ME go get it.) He stood there without moving, and thinking. After taking two slow and deliberate steps in the direction of the marsh, he glanced over his shoulder and gave me that look again.

When I was little, I remember my mother giving me that same look. I had spilled my glass of milk across the kitchen table. When I tried to catch the fallen glass, I had knocked over my sister's glass of milk too. Yep. Same look. Cap turned to face me again - and then he lay down with his intense stare piercing into me as if to say:

"YOU go get it!"

Right." I sighed. "Yes, my fault. It was another stupid toss. I'll go get it."

I hesitated for a moment, thinking about that marsh smell that would permeate my shoes and socks, and decided I really should look for the Disc rather than put Cap back in the jeep and head back into town to get another new Disc. We did not have that much time for such stuff.

I waded out into the tall marsh grass in the direction that I had seen the Disc sail, pushing through the wall of grass before me. My running shoes quickly soaking up the warm marshy water as I waded deep into the fen. Cap splashed along behind me, tight to my heels, not wanting to lose sight of me.

I was mistaken about the marsh grass being eight feet tall. It was clearly at least ten feet tall. Thirty feet into the marsh with the water nearly up to my knees, I began thinking about leeches, and water moccasins. I wondered if it was possible that I could step into a particularly soggy spot and sink up to my hips in the muck – or trip over something beneath the surface and do a face plant right into the stagnant water...

Cap veered off to the right to search while I continued to push ahead in the direction of the Disc. Parting the grass as I slowly and carefully stepped deeper into the dense grass, I hunted for his beloved Disc.

A bright pink Disc should be very easy to spot on a sunny day like today, I though optimistically. I wandered about in the marsh, skirting a floating patch of greenish tan stuff that was slightly frothy on top, and turned back toward the general direction in which I had come.

"Wait . . . this isn't the direction I came from. That's the direction I came from."

The lone cottonwood to the west sent bits of fluff floating on the gentle breeze high above the tassels on the marsh grass, and I oriented myself correctly. I just couldn't help but think about another day not unlike this, when three of my running buddies and myself had decided that we would go to Lapham Peak where there was going to be a beginner's class on Orienteering.

"Cool, this will be fun!" We thought to ourselves.

Each of us had purchased a compass because we heard you needed one of those things. I had asked my husband the night before:

"How does this work?" And I got that look again.

"You don't know how to use a compass?!"

"Of course not. I've never even held one in my hands before. And I live in a small town. I know where I am."

We never did take that Orienteering class . . . um . . . because we could not find the place where they were meeting.

Out of the corner of my eye, I spotted bright pink. Yes!! There it was: laying on edge propped up against the base of a thick clump of the grass. I picked up the Disc and waded back toward the narrow ribbon of a watery path that Cap had created from his many trips into the marsh to cool himself off.

"I found it, Cap! Let's get out of here!"

Twenty feet to the east, Cap stood there frozen in position, staring at something on the opposite side of another thick clump of marsh grass. What could it be? Water moccasin? Muskrat? Perhaps some other idiot who can't throw a Disc and could not find his way out of the marsh?

If it was something like a snake, Cap has a lot more speed than I do, and he might just scare the thing off. Unless, of course, his herding instinct should kick in – and he felt compelled to herd whatever it was directly over to me!

Cap has a high prey drive, it was entirely possible that whatever he had locked on to was alive, fast, and not something we should be messing around with. Feeling just ever so slightly apprehensive, I cautiously waded over to Cap and came up behind him to see what he had locked on.

It was the brand new bright orange Disc. The one I had tossed out there last week and had lost.

Now, if we could just find the white glow-in-the-dark one . . .

Little Pieces

Melanie sat on the floor, unable to sit straight and tall like her mother had always admonished her to do when she was a child. Today, it would be impossible. And tomorrow . . . it probably would not be possible then either.

Her mind was too busy thinking about the dog that lay across her lap. When he came to be with her, he had no name. She remembered that day very well. The first sight of him was enough to break her heart into little pieces.

The woman, who had taken this dog from the rough streets where he had lived, had tried to save him because she was unable to watch this young dog find his own food in a dumpster outside the crack house where he lived.

Nobody cared that he was gone. His fur was very thick, so thick that she had to wiggle her fingers down to feel his bony body. And as she pulled her fingers away again, they were coated in old dirt. Black and white, he was supposed to be. But on that day, he was beige and dust.

179

A Perfectly Good Dog

He sat in the back of her car panting continuously, ears laid outward for he had lost his courage and could not keep them proud and tall. He sat motionless, waiting and limp.

But the thing that was the most disturbing was the look in his eyes. They were quiet eyes, sunken into his head - and they watched her. They were alive with thought. He was waiting for her to do something "to" him. Little did he know at the time that, instead, she would "give" something to him.

She gave him one of the little broken pieces of her heart. She reached out to stroke his head and he instinctively squinched his eyes shut and dropped his head, waiting for the heavy hand. With that little bit of movement, she gave him another one of the broken pieces of her heart.

She took him home and gave him a bath. She toweled him dry and brushed some order back into his coat. For that, he was grateful and even though his own heart was loaded with worms, he accepted yet another piece of her heart, for it would help to heal his own.

"Would you like some water, big boy?" She whispered to him as she set down a large bowl of cold well water.

He drank it up happily. He had been dehydrated for a long time and she knew it would take him most of the week to re-hydrate. He wanted more water - but it was gone.

"Ah...that is how it is," he thought to himself. But he was grateful for what he had been able to get.

"Would you like some more?" and she gave him another bowl along with another little piece of her heart. "I know that you are hungry. You don't have to find your own food anymore. Here is a big bowl of good food for you. I've added some warm water and a little piece of my heart."

Over the four months that he stayed with her, his health improved. The heart full of worms was replaced piece by piece with little bits of her loving heart. And each little piece worked a very special kind of magic.

When the warmth of love and gentle caresses are added, the little broken pieces knit together again and heal the container it resides in. That container becomes whole again.

She watched each little broken piece fill a gap in the gentle dog until his quiet eyes radiated the light from the little pieces. You see, kind words gently spoken turn the little pieces into illumination for the spirit that resides within. He rested beside her, happy to be with her always. Never had he known such kindness, such gentle caresses, such love.

His health had returned, his spirit was playful - as a young dog's should be and he had learned about love. Now his heart was full. The healing was complete. It was time to go. There was another person who had another heart that was meant to be shared with him.

So, she sat shapeless on the floor because all the broken pieces of her heart were with the dog. It is difficult to sit tall when your heart is not with you.

She wrapped her arms around the dog that sat with tall, proud ears for her.

"Lean on me," he said.

She gave him one last thing that would keep him strong - that would keep the pieces of her heart together long after he had gone on to live his new life. She gave him her tears and bound them to the pieces with a simple statement made from the ribbons of her heart.

"I love you, Joe." And Joe lived happily ever after.

Melanie sat on the floor, straight and tall like her mother had always admonished her to do when she was a child. Today, it would be possible. And tomorrow.... it probably would be possible too. Because her mind was busy thinking about this, the next dog that lay across her lap.

Where did she get the heart to help yet another dog, you ask. Ahh . . . it came with the dog. They always bring a little bit of heart with them. And when the rescuer breathes in that little bit of heart, it quickly grows and fills the void left by the last dog.

A Perfectly Good Dog

Printed in the United States
38674LVS00003B/93